Action-Packed

2nd Edition

Packed

CLASSROOMS, K–5

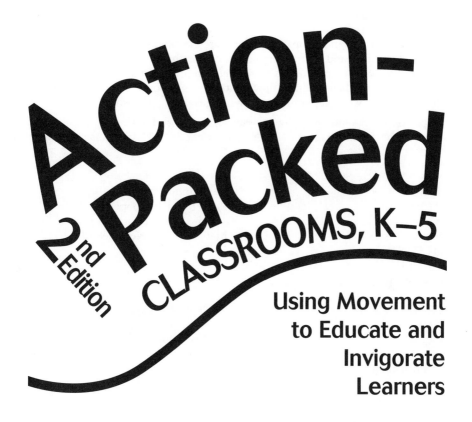

Action-Packed

2nd Edition

CLASSROOMS, K–5

Using Movement
to Educate and
Invigorate
Learners

Cathie
Summerford

Foreword by **John Joseph Ratey**

CORWIN
A SAGE Company

Credits: Photographs on the opening pages of Chapters 1, 2, 3, 4, and 6, Copyright © Jean-Michel Comet. Photograph on the opening page of Chapter 5, Copyright © 2005 Jupiter Images Corporation.

For information:

Corwin
A SAGE Company
2455 Teller Road
Thousand Oaks, California 91320
(800) 233-9936
Fax: (800) 417-2466
www.corwinpress.com

SAGE India Pvt. Ltd.
B 1/I 1 Mohan Cooperative
    Industrial Area
Mathura Road, New Delhi 110 044
India

SAGE Ltd.
1 Oliver's Yard
55 City Road
London EC1Y 1SP
United Kingdom

SAGE Asia-Pacific Pte. Ltd.
33 Pekin Street #02-01
Far East Square
Singapore 048763

Printed in the United States of America

Library of Congress Cataloging-in-Publication Data

Summerford, Cathie, 1957–
Action-packed classrooms, K–5 : using movement to educate and invigorate learners/Cathie Summerford ; foreword by John Joseph Ratey.
— 2nd ed.
    p. cm.
Includes bibliographical references.
ISBN 978-1-4129-7090-7 (cloth : acid-free paper)
ISBN 978-1-4129-7091-4 (pbk. : acid-free paper)
    1. Movement education. 2. Learning—Physiological aspects. 3. Cognition in children.
I. Title.

GV452.S76 2009
372.86'8—dc22   2008042304

This book is printed on acid-free paper.

09   10   11   12   13   10   9   8   7   6   5   4   3   2

Acquisitions Editor:	Jessica Allan
Editorial Assistant:	Joanna Coelho
Production Editor:	Jane Haenel
Copy Editor:	Amy Rosenstein
Typesetter:	C&M Digitals (P) Ltd.
Proofreader:	Gail Fay
Cover Designer:	Lisa Riley
Graphic Designer:	Karine Hovsepian

Contents

Foreword

Cathie Summerford begins at the beginning, taking us into the world of the jam-packed classroom, wondering how teachers find the time to add movement to the many things they want to accomplish. There is no support or reward for it, and there is the danger that their charges will not pass their state exams. Cathie focuses first on grabbing students' attention system—entering movement into the mix forces students' attention to switch focus, the first step in transforming a classroom into one that is action packed, and prepares students for learning. She offers many practical examples and strategies to pick up the pace in the classroom. She explores games and ways of presenting material that sound as though teachers and students are racing through the streets in the Boston marathon. Her philosophy is that moving is living and sitting is not. This is happening all over the place. Our world needs to plan a reaction against our sedentary existence. There are now eager and serious moves to bring movement into the workplace; the *Harvard Business Review* in February 2008 had a section called "10 Breakthrough Ideas for 2008," and one of them was a three-page cartoon called "The Boardroom of the Future." Instead of sitting in chairs, 10 board members are moving on treadmills as they plan their company's future. The "tread desk" is already being sold, and soon we will have chairs that keep us moving to keep our brains at their peak. Current health research examines how much our brains need our bodies to be in motion.

Cathie carries the enthusiasm to recess, not apologizing for the task of exercising but seeing it as a real opportunity to prepare the brain for learning. No doubt keeping things flying in the classroom will grab students' attention, but making them run and play during recess or physical education will improve the learner in a few important ways. By getting the students to spend enough time in their aerobic zone, you immediately increase the release of neurotransmitters. Exercise causes a burst of dopamine, norepinephrine, and serotonin to be released in the brain; thus, a bout of exercise is like taking a little bit of Prozac and a little bit of Ritalin just at the right places in the brain. This leads to a happy set of consequences: the student is more focused, less distractible, and more positive; has more energy and a sense of vigor; and has a decrease in impulsiveness that shows as a decrease in restlessness. Students will also be more prepared to overcome what we in mental health call "learned helplessness," an attitude that comes with chronic failure. They are quicker to explore and are more motivated. All this, and students have optimized their neurons to be ready to do their job. The nerve cells involved in learning have to "wire" together, meaning they have to bind and change, yes, actually change, to learn. Exercise prepares the environment for the brain to change better than anything else we know of because exercise also releases a chemical that I call Miracle-Gro, or brain fertilizer. Stimulated by movement, this chemical does exactly what fertilizer does on the ground—it makes things grow easier, be healthier, and last longer. The science world also is abuzz over neurogenesis, the idea that exercise is best at helping us add new neurons to the ones we have. We are making new brain cells daily, and if we keep our children moving, we might be making more possibilities for them now and in the future.

Cathie's book can help you keep the process of neuroplasticity moving optimally. By keeping students moving, you are helping their brains prepare to learn.

—*John Joseph Ratey*
Harvard University

Author's Welcome

Welcome to our second edition of *Action-Packed Classrooms*. I am confident it will have an incredibly positive impact on your teaching and your students' learning. There is no honor greater than to touch the direction and potential of one's life. This is especially true in education, when children are the most impressionable.

Action and movement stimulate the body, which in turn stimulates the brain and, hence, one's ability to learn and retain information. *Action-Packed Classrooms* is based on research well documented in this book and is based on clear objectives for standards-based instruction. If you can bring energy into your classroom, your students will be motivated and invigorated to retain more information.

The strategies and techniques presented in *Action-Packed Classroom* should become a standard requirement in all classrooms, schools, and school districts globally. The research is done, the case studies are complete, and the results are in—bringing movement and music into the classroom works! Engaging multiple modalities reaches more of our learners.

This edition is loaded with Action-Packed Template Games, Fit4Learning A.C.T.I.V.E. Standards, updated brain research with an incredible timeline, and more, along with our tried-and-true original activities. It's a no-brainer; you and your students will enjoy the active learning.

You will soon learn how easy it is to bring movement and music into your classroom. As you master the *Action-Packed Classrooms* teaching strategies and techniques, my hope is that you stay on target with these awesome classroom-engaging ideas. So, here's the deal. I have developed and enclosed a commitment agreement between you, your principal, and myself to do all that we can to support you in bringing Action-Packed Lessons into your classroom to achieve optimum learning with your students. This journey is not a solo journey; it is a team effort to internalize action into your teaching style for optimal learning. You are not alone.

So, ready, set, action! Team up with another teacher or your whole school to implement *Action-Packed Classrooms* to make sure that the skills you master will become an inherent part of your teaching style and culture. Embrace the *Action-Packed Classroom* teaching techniques as you will find the joy once again in teaching and learning—you can't go wrong!

Finally, remember to pledge this school year with the commitment contract. It is a great way to start your year off right. Study the *Action-Packed Classrooms* techniques and apply them in your lesson plans, and watch the test scores of your students grow. Good luck and have fun!

—*Cathie Summerford*

Action-Packed Classrooms Commitment Contract

On the _____ day, of _____, 20___, We the undersigned agree to the best of our abilities in providing for our students an optimal academic classroom that motivates and invigorates the learning process. We will take these Action-Packed Classroom strategies embracing standards-based instruction that is exciting and engaging for the success of all students. We want our students to love learning.

_____   _____
Principal   Teacher

Cathie Summerford
Author

www.FIT4LEARNING.com

Acknowledgments

Corwin would like to thank the following peer reviewers for their editorial insight and guidance:

Stephanie Eagleton
Second-Grade Teacher
Shaker Heights City School District
Shaker Heights, OH

Debbie Jo Halcomb
Fourth-Grade Teacher
Robert W. Combs Elementary School
Happy, KY

Sharon Jefferies, MEd, NBCT
Orange County Public Schools
Orlando, FL

Marcia LeCompte
Fifth-Grade Teacher
Belfair Elementary School
Baton Rouge, LA

Debbie Smith
Master Teacher
Lady's Island Elementary School
Beaufort, SC

Andrea Ziemba
Fifth-Grade Teacher
Morton Elementary School
Hammond, IN

About the Author

Cathie Summerford, MS, has engaged learners internationally with action, movement, and music in her dynamic keynotes and workshops. Recognized as a true trailblazer and outstanding author in her field, Cathie takes an energetic, action-packed approach to teaching that has livened up learning in countless classrooms globally.

Along with this second edition *Action-Packed Classrooms,* she also authored *PE-4-ME: Teaching Lifelong Health and Fitness* and is cited in numerous national articles and journals. As an Educational Consultant and President of Fit4Learning, Cathie has been recognized as a California Teacher of the Year, a National Association of Sport and Physical Education Teacher of the Year, and California School Boards Association (CSBA) Golden Bell award-winning author.

Cathie's experiences in the academic classroom and the physical education arena have provided her with ideas galore to share with others. She continually motivates teachers to make learning a meaningful and exciting experience. Cathie's expertise in brain research and the implications action has on learning combined with her enthusiasm for teaching children make her an excellent source for inspiration; she has tons of ideas at her fingertips and is ready and eager to share this knowledge and enthusiasm with others.

Cathie's rapid-fire presentations focus on involvement. They move quickly, cover a lot of ground, and actively engage the participants. As a result, teachers leave her workshops with dozens of practical ideas and with a renewed love for teaching!

In addition, she has more than 19 years of quality experience teaching all levels, from preschool children to college-age students. Her tried-and-true activities are "kid-proof" and "adult-friendly" and are loads of fun. On top of that, she is a two-time Ironman Triathlon finisher!

Thank You, God, for allowing me to be Your vehicle through Action-Packed Classrooms. *I am truly blessed.*

Action-Packed Classrooms *is written in honor and as a tribute to all teachers who are out in the trenches making a difference in the lives of kids. There is no other profession that has such a lasting impact on children.*

For you, MAG, as a tribute for all that you contribute, support, and give. Our friendship means the world to me.

Action-Packed Classrooms *is dedicated to Thomas M. Nichols. Without his continual love, support, and guidance pertaining to Fit4Learning and particularly to this Action-Packed project, I couldn't have done it. I love you, Thomas.*

Introduction

The latest research shows that for your brain to function at its peak,
your body needs to move.

—John Joseph Ratey, MD

The state of public education has been the subject of consternation for many decades and the standards-/assessment-driven movement of the current administration is only the most recent of many attempts by officials to try and effect change in a distressed system. However, the question that needs answering is not how to motivate teachers to teach, but how should they teach in order for children to learn? Or, more pointedly, how do children learn and, therefore, making use of the diverse resources at our disposal, how should we teach? In an effort to utilize cutting-edge educational research, this book will apply the latest in brain-based research to show the effectiveness of creating an action-packed classroom for the success of all learners.

BENEFITS OF ACTION-PACKED CLASSROOMS

1. To understand the research behind exercise, movement, and learning

2. To learn strategies to anchor learning in any classroom

3. To gain knowledge of movement-based activities for intrinsic learning

4. To create an action plan to immediately implement in any classroom

Brain-based research has been the subject of scientific study since the mid-1800s, when Hitzig and Fritsch (1870) first discovered that the areas of the brain responsible for movement could be located in the cerebral cortex. However, the results of this fascinating field of research, which have such diverse applications in the field of education, have not found their way into general practice. The current educational system is not making effective use of the resources available nor putting into practice the volumes of relevant research that could make a difference in what our children learn.

This country has developed a very rich, visual, mobile, multicultural society with readily available access to cutting-edge research in scientific fields. Brain research demonstrates that our bodies and brains are inherently connected and that no single organ has one unilateral purpose. The old vision of a seeing eye and understanding brain are really just an archaic myth that has been replaced by what we now recognize as a perceiving individual (Kindler, 2003). Our culture is cultivating the active-spatial sense of our people, but schools are still failing to make full use of moving mediums in instructional practice.

Most recently, studies of brain-based learning have shown that exercise can increase cognitive ability in children. This has specific applications for the field of education and draws into discussion such questions as how an increasingly sedentary lifestyle in this country is affecting its youth.

Despite the extraordinary quantity and quality of brain-based research that calls for motion activities to be utilized in the instructional setting, these types of activities are not being consistently implemented in classroom practice. The purpose of *Action-Packed Classrooms* is to show that research supports best practices that merge movement into the academic classroom that will employ these methods. The lessons, strategies, ideas, and game plans presented in this book are easy to implement and will help ensure that research finally finds a consistent place in education. In addition, we will explore the overwhelming benefits of aerobic activity on our brains. Ready, set, go!

Action-Packed Classrooms is divided into these main sections:

- Understanding the effect of exercise and movement on learning
- Developing kinesthetic teaching strategies linking core content
- Developing an action plan . . . the how-tos

As you travel through the first part of the book, you will learn about incorporating movement into the classroom. Next, you will get a primer on the body and the brain along with an incredible research timeline, which contains information vital to making sense of what research says regarding movement in the classroom.

Continuing along, you will discover incredible strategies for developing kinesthetic lessons for your classroom. Anchoring learning through procedural processes, you will learn how exciting and fun the learning experience can be for your students.

Next, you will learn how to put together an action plan. In our standards-based world, how can we jump-start learning when kids are so burned out on "the testing game?" No problem here! *Action-Packed Classrooms* is taking learning to a new level. This is not your typical classroom teacher book; the energy you will feel from the text will be flying off the pages ready to "make it happen" in your classroom.

Action-Packed Classrooms **Flow Chart**

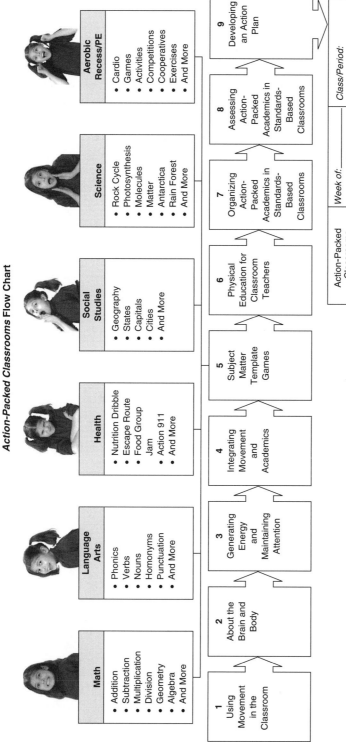

Math
- Addition
- Subtraction
- Multiplication
- Division
- Geometry
- Algebra
- And More

Language Arts
- Phonics
- Verbs
- Nouns
- Homonyms
- Punctuation
- And More

Health
- Nutrition Dribble
- Escape Route
- Food Group Jam
- Action 911
- And More

Social Studies
- Geography
- States
- Capitals
- Cities
- And More

Science
- Rock Cycle
- Photosynthesis
- Molecules
- Matter
- Antarctica
- Rain Forest
- And More

Aerobic Recess/PE
- Cardio
- Games
- Activities
- Competitions
- Cooperatives
- Exercises
- And More

1 Using Movement in the Classroom

2 About the Brain and Body

3 Generating Energy and Maintaining Attention

4 Integrating Movement and Academics

5 Subject Matter Template Games

6 Physical Education for Classroom Teachers

7 Organizing Action-Packed Academics in Standards-Based Classrooms

8 Assessing Action-Packed Academics in Standards-Based Classrooms

9 Developing an Action Plan

Action-Packed Classrooms Weekly Action Plan	*Week of:* _____ *to* _____				*Class/Period:*	
Day	Academic Integration	Music	Activities	Games	State Changes	Energizers
M						
T						
W						
TH						
F						

Implementation

3

This book is a one-stop resource to enliven learning in any classroom. *Action-Packed Classrooms* will follow the flow of the preceding chart and will travel through the disciplines, focusing on the following:

- Setting goals for more action
- Describing the brain and the body/key research
- Developing kinesthetic teaching strategies
- Developing an action plan
- Organizing standards-based classrooms
- Assessing standards-based classrooms
- Implementing your plan

At the conclusion of this book, you will be filled with a wealth of information and tools to fire up your classroom and to bring learning alive.

Using Movement in the Classroom

All glory comes from daring to begin.

—William Shakespeare

LET'S BEGIN

Depending on your objective, movement can be used in a variety of venues, ranging from calming the environment to creating an adrenaline rush to simply transitioning students from one lesson or activity to another. Movement can be expressed and described by being less active or very active, depending on the purpose and the intensity of the activity and the objective of the lesson. The focus will be to figure out just when and how much movement is appropriate in different learning situations, and the effects it has on academic retention. We will examine the differences of movement, physical activity, and exercise and determine the effect that different activities, from a slight movement to a high-impact aerobic type of activity, have on the brain in terms of academic performance. Perhaps of most interest to teachers, this chapter will clarify the confusion that is often associated with movement in the classroom and explain why it is so essential in education.

CHECK THIS OUT

Mrs. Wilson, a fourth-grade teacher in Fontana, California, prepares for yet another lesson at Coleman Elementary School. Her day is never dull; she teaches math, language arts, science, social studies, and physical education (PE) along with recess duty. All of this stuff to do, and no time to fit it all in! Who really has time to teach PE anyways when the emphasis is on standardized testing? "When every minute counts, there just isn't any time for frill," she says to herself as she frantically gets materials together for the children. Often she has to ask herself, "How can I possibly fit all of this into a day and cover all of the standards that need to be taught, not just covered, for the state of California? And if it's not on the test, why cover it?"

On top of that, the 28 students that she teaches are very diverse as they come from many cultures and backgrounds. More than 50% are Hispanic, approximately 20% are African American, 8% are of Asian descent, and the remaining students are a mix of all other ethnicities. Two Hispanic students don't speak English, and many of the students are classified as attention deficit disorder (ADD)/attention deficit hyperactivity disorder (ADHD) and are a nightmare to keep on task.

Mrs. Wilson has come to the conclusion that if she can just keep them in their seats, focused on their work, and quiet, then mission accomplished! The thought of them getting up, moving around, and doing stuff only presents a vision of chaos. Mrs. Wilson does not want to lose control of what she is "used to doing" and teach out of her comfort zone. This is how she has done things for more than 20 years!

But one has to ask, is this really an effective strategy for learning? Are kids engaged in the learning process? And are there more successful and fun approaches to teaching and learning?

Take a moment to reflect on the "Mrs. Wilsons" at your school. Can you relate? Are there teachers experiencing a similar situation, or are you that teacher? As you read on, you will discover that movement in the academic classroom is essential to keeping kids focused, excited, enthused, and ready to learn, and you don't have to lose control of your class. Our brains and bodies are not designed to sit down, shut up, and stay focused for hours on end. Your choice in planning with more action, when to use it, and how to "make it happen" will be a delightful addition to your academic learning environment.

WHY EVEN BOTHER?

Before you begin the process of planning, there needs to be a thorough understanding of what the purpose of movement is in the classroom. When do you use movement? Why? What are the different levels of movement? What is whole body-brain activation? And why is aerobic activity even mentioned in this book? Classroom teachers are not PE teachers! Don't worry; as you sink yourself into this section of the book, you will discover just how important it is to get those brains ready for prime learning and how aerobic exercise is an awesome component of teaching that sets the stage.

MOVEMENT FACILITATES COGNITION

- Movement anchors learning through the body.
- Movement energizes and integrates the body and brain for optimal learning.
- Movement makes learning fun.

Movement Anchors Learning Through the Body

Just imagine, learning the multiplication facts or action words such as verbs by using your body. Doesn't that sound like a lot more fun than just sitting there? Most important, the facts and information are a part of your entire body. Through procedural memory, by doing, you learn. How does this work? The body is full of peptides and cells throughout that become engaged and have a memory of their own. Once it's in your body, you don't forget it! When kids learn about verbs by moving to the action word, hearing the music, and acting out the word with their bodies, they get it!

Movement Energizes and Integrates the Body and Brain for Optimal Learning

Just as an artist needs to prepare the canvas for a masterpiece, teachers need to prepare their children in their classrooms for optimal learning. Each child is a bud on a bush ready to blossom; we as teachers just need to plant the seeds, but, most important, nourish the seeds with some energy and fuel that use the whole child. That is the only way children can grow!

What would be an effective strategy to prepare the kids for "what's coming up next" as you prepare your game plan? How can you include enthusiasm and excitement in the lessons and still keep students on task? With energizers, attention grabbers, jump starters, and cooperative games, students are ready for learning as the teacher now has their attention. Core concepts are included in the energizers. Learning is now integrated into action-based activities. New and novel goings-on leave no room for the ugly villain boredom.

Movement Makes Learning Fun

What student could possibly be bored when learning is fun? Add fun to the curriculum, and teachers will have happy campers. Think back when you were a kid (okay, you still are); what were the most fun activities in your various classes? Usually, what comes to mind are lessons where there was action or movement incorporated. Why? Because kids need to move!

Of great concern is the obesity issue skyrocketing and affecting our children. Because of a lack of activity in the lifestyles of many kids, moving around is a great effort. Laziness may be a factor. To address these issues, (1) get them involved in active learning at earlier ages, and (2) make sure the energizers are not threatening, as some kids are not quite as active as others. Activities need to be all-inclusive.

DIFFERENTIATE WHEN AND WHY TO INCLUDE MOVEMENT

There are many reasons to include movement into your classroom. There are many differentiations when to include it. Figure 1.1 is a very simplified approach to this goal.

When reviewing the graphic organizer in Figure 1.1, we can see that there is a time and place to "get 'em movin'." At times, it is advantageous to arouse learners with an old-fashioned dose of jamming tunes and vigorous moves to get them engaged; at other times, students need to relax and focus. Let's take a look at the differences and see what the different outcomes may be.

1. **Grab Attention:** Have you ever had students in your class who may have been there physically, but you're just not sure if they are there mentally? This is when it's a good time to "grab their attention." This can be done by having students change seats, point to an object in the room, or perform a basic pencil roll. Grabbing attention is the same as getting them focused.

2. **Energize and Engage:** To energize and engage is to get the learners involved in the learning process by creating enthusiasm and motivation for their own learning. If students are not interested or do not take ownership in their education, they shut down and turn off to learning.

3. **Relax and Focus:** There are occasions when it is beneficial to calm down and relax before the students progress to the next lesson. Movement can provide super benefits for accomplishing this goal. Holding cross-lateral positions while listening to soothing music is just one idea.

The quantity of movement depends on your objective and the age of the students. For example, youngsters are very active in general and need frequent opportunities to move, while older students may need longer durations of an exercise but at intervals that are not as frequent. Each group of learners and situations is different. The instructor must be able to read the students and to adjust the movement accordingly.

Another important use of movement is transitioning children from one lesson to another. When done effectively, transitioning creates a seamless flow of great teaching interwoven with activity in a traditional classroom

Figure 1.1   Attention

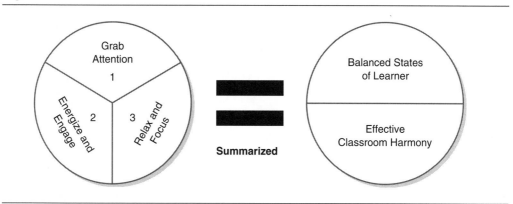

environment. For example, once kids have finished a written test, the teacher could turn the process of handing in test papers into an activity. "In 10 seconds, when I say go, grab your test, stand up . . . go!" Play music. Pause. "If you would please, take 10 giant steps in any direction, give your test paper to the closest person . . . go!" Play music. Pause. "People with tests walk forward in any direction and drop the tests in the basket; testless people walk backward in any direction . . . go!" Play music. Pause.

Yippee! Not only did you as the teacher collect the assignments in a fun, active way, the students had fun doing it, and they finally got to move after working for so long on the grueling test.

WHAT ARE THE DIFFERENCES OF MOVEMENT?

As a classroom teacher, you need to understand what the differences of movement are and how they apply to academic instructors. Each component of movement is a huge part in the educational process. The evidence is clear: understanding movement before implementing it is vital to success.

Figure 1.2 does a great job of defining the differences of movement.

1. **Movement:** Not being stationary. For example, just the act of standing up out of a chair raises the heart rate, which changes the state of the learner. Moving the body (transitioning) from one place to another is another example of movement.

2. **Physical Activity:** Best described as a voluntary movement that is more involved than basic movement. When we are physically active in a classroom, we are exposed to great opportunities to anchor learning through the activity.

3. **Exercise:** Raising the heart rate into the target heart rate zone for a minimum of 20 minutes, ideally three times per week, if not more.

Figure 1.2   Optimal Learning

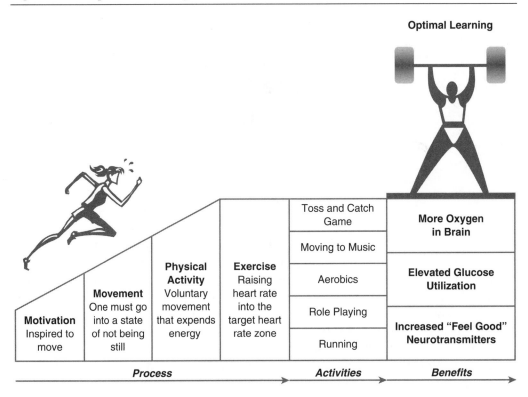

Instructional methods should alternate repetitive sedentary activities with more pleasurable, movement-orientated activities because our brain's attentional system is set up to prefer high contrast, originality, and exciting connotations. Instead of force-feeding dull and ineffective content, instruction should take a cue from research and include more stimulating, interactive material.

Neuroscience is discovering at a dizzying rate that aerobic exercise is absolutely necessary for our brains to function at top condition. Scientists are demonstrating in study after study all over the world that, at the neuronal and cellular level, our brains are designed for and need aerobic, voluntary exercising activities to function at optimal levels. With such great emphasis placed on standardized testing, doesn't it make sense to get students' brains in top condition? Instead of focusing on test-taking strategies, doesn't it behoove learners to "clean the slate in their brains" and remove all of the clutter? With more oxygen to the brain, neurotransmitters rockin' and rollin', and the brain nourishment for the neurons optimized to do their thing, wouldn't it be advantageous for us classroom teachers to take this "exercise thing" a bit more serious? Absolutely! It's as easy as 1, 2, 3 (see Figure 1.3).

Figure 1.3   1, 2, 3

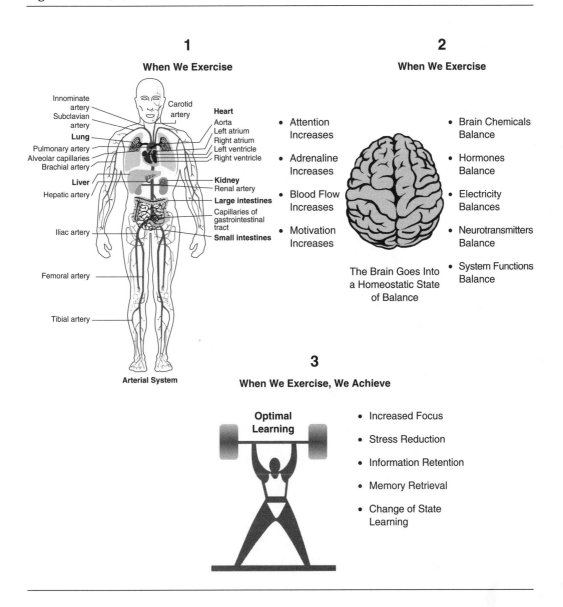

When we exercise, the body goes into high gear. Attention, adrenaline, blood flow, and motivation are elevated. This creates a balanced or homeostatic state in the learner. Why is the brain balanced? Because of the increase of brain chemicals, hormones, electricity, and neurotransmitters, the entire neural system functions more efficiently. What are the benefits of a homeostatic brain? Better retention, stress reduction, increased memory retrieval, state change, and a more focused student. How do you get these benefits? By aerobic recess activities, quality physical education, and athletics.

1. **Warm-Up:** Preparing the body-brain for exercise.

2. **Fat Burning Zone:** Reached just before a participant reaches their target heart rate. Everyone is different, so each person's fat burning zone varies. A ballpark number would be 130 beats per minute.

3. **Heart Rate Zone:** Raising the heart rate into the aerobic zone for a minimum of 20 minutes, ideally three times per week, if not more. The positive benefits of aerobic exercise and the impact on the brain for optimal learning are impressive.

A highly recommended book is Dr. John Ratey's *Spark: The Revolutionary New Science of Exercise and the Brain* for an in-depth understanding of the science of exercise. This book is a must-read for administrators, superintendents, politicians, teachers, and change agents. Visit www.johnratey.com for more information.

It has been demonstrated that activity is necessary to gain knowledge; because each individual comprehends and participates in a distinctive way, it is impossible to plan a single activity, engaging a specific method and predicting a patterned response, and still expect that all students will learn. Because an individual's brain changes physiologically as a result of the individual's unique experiences, it is impossible even to predict from day to day which singular activity might prove successful. Instruction must be diverse if it is to capture the attention of each member of a diverse group of students.

It is important for academic growth and individual well-being that instruction cultivates a child's intelligence, not the static number provided by standardized tests but a wide-ranging set of multiple competencies. Students need to be taught that there are learning preferences in the way the brain receives, processes, and expresses information so that they can recognize themselves as normal and validate their learning methods.

WHOLE BODY-BRAIN ACTIVATION

Although classroom teachers might be tempted at times, it is not possible (or appropriate!) for teachers to take off their students' heads and pour the information into them. Why do they need the rest of their bodies anyway? The body only gets in the way as the kids become too distractive and hyper by wiggling and shuffling around. Why doesn't the information poured into these students' heads stick? Where is it all going? Many a teacher is amazed that even after going over and over the material with students, they still don't get it. Weren't these the same little darlings that were in class day in and day out? Yikes!

Whether you like it or not, the body has to be included for true learning to occur. The body is not the largest part of our beings for nothing; we need to use it! Let's take a look at whole body-brain activation.

Figure 1.4   Mind, Body, and Spirit

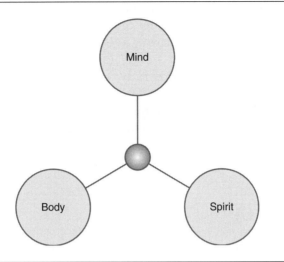

Figure 1.4 is excellent at demonstrating the importance of the integral entanglement and connection of the mind, body, and spirit. One does not operate or function without the other. Working in unison and hopefully for one common goal in the educational arena, the mind, body, and spirit far exceed the capabilities of the most advanced computer programs. When functioning in full capacity, the mind, body, and spirit can overcome impossibilities for those hard-to-reach learners. The human being is capable of amazing challenges when the whole is tapped into.

- **Mind:** The mind, or brain, is located at the top of our heads (hopefully). We as instructor need to capitalize on its maximum efficiency.
- **Body:** The body comprises many vital organs and systems, including the brain; it's the part that gets hyper and can drive a teacher crazy.
- **Spirit:** The spirit is the internal driving force that makes each one of us who we are from the core of our being. Without delving into religion or too much detail, let's just say it is our soul and operates in our minds and bodies.

No ifs, ands, or buts—in education we have to include all three dimensions into academia. Human beings are put together with a mind, a body, and a spirit for a reason. The whole is greater than the sum of its parts. Use it or lose it!

MAKE IT HAPPEN

Now that the writing is on the wall and the evidence is in, without a shadow of a doubt, it's time as teachers to get moving in our classrooms! The critical information needed to make sense in planning is superbly explained and is coming up in future pages. The following chapters will suffice the mission of "just doing it." Chapters 4 through 7 include all of the activities, energizers, and attention grabbers to get movin' and groovin'. Chapter 8 will get you organized, and Chapter 9 will keep you up-to-speed in assessment. In the meantime, the "Make-It-Happen Checklist for Movement in Your Classroom" (see Resources) is an excellent checklist to add movement to your classroom. By completing and filling out activities for A, B, and C, you can check to see that you have included movement into your classroom. With this checklist, you can monitor whether you are on target in your quest to liven up your classroom. Remember to start with baby steps and add more activity when you are feeling more comfortable. This should be a joyful, fun process for you.

LET'S WRAP IT UP

It has been established that activity is necessary to gain knowledge, and, because each individual comprehends and participates in a distinctive way, it is impossible to plan a single lesson that suffices for every child every day at the same time.

It has been decisively and consistently demonstrated that movement has significant impact on thinking and learning by anchoring an individual's thoughts and providing a framework for developmental processes. Body-centered learning that incorporates cadence, music, energizers, attention grabbers, and aerobic recess/physical education activities should be routinely included in instruction, and, yes, for academic teachers. Integrating subject learning with active learning should be an ongoing strategy that collaborating teachers use to maximum opportunities for students to learn content-area information.

Given the increasing numbers of students with ADD and learning disabilities, groups that are often highly medicated for movement issues, it is irresponsible to ignore data that many children who have been identified with attention problems have hypokinesis. Even more so than their peers, children with ADD and children with learning and mental disabilities need learning programs that incorporate movement into classroom instruction.

Students who are taught that learning truly can be fun will be anxious and ready for the next learning lesson. When students are engaged fully, the whole mind/body/spirit, into the academic learning classroom, nothing but magic will occur. The students will be there, ready and willing, to tackle any new challenge.

Not only will the students enjoy their education more, but teachers will have more fun to boot! So, to all of the Mrs. Wilsons out there, let's make it happen in your classroom and fire up learning.

About the Brain and Body

The goal of education is to replace an empty mind with an open mind.

—Malcolm Forbes

LET'S BEGIN

Information about neuroscience, with its subsequent implications on education, has exploded in recent years. Technology's rapid pace has allowed scientists to bring to the educational forefront the research behind the science of how our brains work and how we as humans learn. The following facts are some "blow you away" bits of information that give educators background about the amazing brain and the integration of our entire bodies.

CHECK THIS OUT

Have you heard about the next planned *Survivor* television show? Three businessmen and three businesswomen will be placed in an elementary school in a New York City classroom for six weeks. Each professional will be provided with a copy of his or her school district's curriculum and will have to teach a class of 28 students. Each class will have five students with learning disabilities, three students with attention deficit disorder, one gifted student, and two students who speak limited English. Three students will be labeled with severe behavior problems.

The professionals must complete lesson plans at least three days in advance with annotations for curriculum objectives, and they must modify, organize, or create materials accordingly. They will be required to teach students, handle misconduct, implement technology, document attendance, write referrals, correct homework, make bulletin boards, compute grades, complete report cards, document benchmarks, communicate with parents, and arrange parent-teacher conferences. Professionals must also supervise recess and monitor the hallways.

In addition, the professionals will complete drills for fire, tornados, and shooting attacks. They must attend workshops (50 minutes twice a week), faculty meetings, union meetings, and curriculum development meetings. They must also tutor those students who are behind and strive to get two non-English-speaking children proficient enough to take the TerraNova and EPA tests.

If the professionals are sick or if they are having a bad day, they must not let it show to students. Each day professionals must incorporate reading, writing, math, science, and social studies into the program. They must maintain discipline and provide an educationally stimulating environment at all times.

The professionals will only have access to the golf course on the weekends, but on their new salary they will not be able to afford that diversion anyway. There will be no access to vendors who want to take them out to lunch, and lunch will be limited to 30 minutes, usually during the only parent phone-call time available. On days when they do not have recess duty, the professionals will be permitted to use the staff restroom as long as another professional is supervising their class.

They will be provided with five 45-minute planning periods per week while their students are at special classes. If the copier is operable, they may make copies of necessary materials during this time. The professionals must continually advance their education on their own time and pay for this advanced training themselves. This can be accomplished by moonlighting at a second job or marrying someone with money.

The winner will be allowed to return to his or her job after release from a sanitarium devoted to treating "shell-shocked" individuals.

WHY EVEN BOTHER?

Teaching is survival of the fittest! As a teacher, to truly survive in education, aside from all of the demands and craziness of a teacher's job description, it is of utmost importance to keep on top of emerging science that addresses how children learn. Although teachers get caught up in the busyness of teaching, when push comes to shove, it all comes down to learning in the classroom. With neuroscience finally meeting up with education, the evidence is clear. What goes on in our brains is important to what goes on in the classroom. This is where the rubber meets the road . . . the pedal meets the metal . . . the axon meets the dendrite!

What is thinking? What is learning? When does learning occur? How does retention of material happen? In this section, we will begin with the body-brain.

What is the body-brain? you ask. We know as educators that the brain is what is in our craniums, and the body is all of the other stuff. So, what *is* body-brain? When discussing the amazing brain or the awesome body, how can we really talk about one without the other? They are entwined, and the research emerging affects both. In regard to *Action-Packed Classrooms*, when thinking about engaging the learning experience, the entire body-brain is involved. When you see this term, think about the impact on the brain as well as the body.

THE BODY-BRAIN: THE ULTIMATE MULTITASKER

The body-brain sets humans apart from all other species by allowing us to achieve the wonders of traveling in space and composing masterpieces of symphonies. Throughout history, the human brain has been compared to a supercomputer. Without a doubt, the brain is the most complex, multitasking organ in the body. This single "thing in our head" controls all body activities, ranging from heart rate and sexual function to emotion, learning, and memory. The brain is even thought to influence the response to disease of the immune system and to determine, in part, how well people respond to medical treatments. It shapes our thoughts, hopes, dreams and imagination: the brain is what makes us human.

Fun Facts

- More than 90% of scientists' knowledge of the brain is garnered from the past five years.
- The brain is comprised of billions and billions of neurons.
- The brain weighs about three pounds, is the size of one half of a cantaloupe, is mushy like an avocado, and is wrinkled like a walnut.
- The brain comprises 2% of the body's weight but uses 20% of the body's energy.
- The brain generates 25 watts of power when a person is awake.
- The brain's neuronal messages travel at speeds of 250 mph.
- The brain processes several billion bits of information each second.
- The brain has about 100,000,000,000 (100 billion) neurons.
- The average brain is 140 mm wide, 167 mm long, and 93 mm high.
- The total surface area of the cerebral cortex is about 2,500 sq cm; the weight of an adult human cerebellum is 150 g.
- If blood supply is cut off to the brain, unconsciousness will occur within 8 to 10 seconds.
- There are 12 pairs of cranial nerves. There are 31 pairs of spinal nerves.
- There are about 13,500,000 neurons in the human spinal cord.
- There are 1,000 to 10,000 synapses for a "typical" neuron.
- The cell bodies of neurons vary in diameter from 4 microns (granule cell) to 100 microns (motor neuron in cord).

As you can see, the body-brain is an astonishing, spongy, three-pound organ that is incredibly busy. From the zillions of neurons in our brains to the volume of cerebrospinal fluid, it truly is a miracle that all of this stuff works! Let's take a look at a timeline of the research.

RESEARCH TIMELINE

1870   E. Hitzig & G. Fritsch

They made the discovery that areas of the brain responsible for movement could be located in the cerebral cortex.

1870   H. Jackson

He suggested the existence of a motor cortex within the cerebral hemispheres.

1973   R. Sperry

He suggested that the brain was a means of refining motor behavior to promote survival instead of motor behaviors existing to support the activity of the brain. (From Neuropsychologia.*)*

1977   J. Streff

He conducted a double-blind study of 538 sixth graders and determined that 30 minutes a day of motor-sensory development lowered test anxiety and incidences of myopia and raised academic success. (From The Chelshire Study: Changes in Incidence of Myopia Following Program of Intervention.*)*

1977   J. Prescott

He noted that the anterior cingulated is particularly active when novel movements or movement combinations are initiated. Also noted that movement impairments negatively affect the cerebellum and its connections to other parts of the brain. (From Phylogenetic and Ontogenetic Aspects of Human Affectional Development.*)*

1977   A. G. Gilbert

He found that third graders studying language arts concepts through dance increased standardized reading scores by 13% in six months. (From Teaching the Three Rs through Movement Experiences.*)*

1980   L. Palmer

He used eye-hand coordination tasks, spinning, tumbling, rocking, pointing, counting, jumping, and ball-toss activities to stimulate early neural growth patterning. (From Academic Therapy.*)*

1980   C. Clarke

His studies suggest that certain spinning activities led to alertness, attention, and relaxation in the classroom. (From Brain/Mind Bulletin.*)*

1980   H. Leiner & A. Leiner

Their research centered on the cerebellum. The cerebellum takes up just one tenth of the brain by volume but contains more than half of all its neurons. It has some 40 million nerve fibers, 40 times more

than even the highly complex optical tract. Those fibers not only feed information from the cortex to the cerebellum, but they feed them back to the cortex. This subsection of the brain, long known for its role in posture, coordination, balance, and movement, may be our brain's sleeping giant.

1982   E. Olsen & F. Martens

In a study of more than 500 Canadian children, students who spent an extra hour each day in gym class performed notably better on exams than less active children. When physical education time was increased to one third of the school day, academic scores went up. (From Journal of Physical Education, Recreation, and Dance.*)*

1986   J. Hooper & D. Teresi

They found that there's a direct link from the cerebellum to the pleasure centers in the emotional system. Kids who enjoy playground games do so for a good reason: sensory-motor experiences feed directly into their brain's pleasure centers. (From The 3-Pound Universe: Revolutionary Discoveries About the Brain From the Chemistry of the Mind to New Frontiers of the Soul.*)*

1986   D. Coulter

The author suggested that long periods of reading without relaxing the focus of the eye by gazing into the distance possibly cause inflammation and the enlargement of the eyeball, leading to myopia or nearsightedness. (From Enter the Child's World.*)*

1989   R. Dienstbier

He suggested that physical exercise alone seems "to train a quick adrenaline-noradrenaline response and rapid recovery." In other words, by working out your body, you'll better train your brain to respond to challenges quickly. (From Psychological Review.*)*

1990   J. E. Black, K. R. Isaacs, B. J. Anderson, A. A. Alcantara, & W. T. Greenbough

The authors found that rats that became proficient at the precise, coordinated movements needed to nimbly run across ropes and thin metal bridges had a greater number of connections among the neurons in their brains than rats that were sedentary or rats that merely ran in automated wheels. In the same way that exercise shapes up the muscles, heart, lungs, and bones, it also strengthens the basal ganglia, cerebellum, and corpus callosum, all key areas of the brain. We know exercise fuels the brain with oxygen, but it also feeds it neurotropins to enhance growth and greater connections between neurons. (From Proceedings of the National Academy of Sciences.*)*

1991   J. Ayers

She discovered a link between touch-sensitivity (inability to tolerate touch) and learning disorders in children. (From Sensory Integration and Learning Disorders.*)*

1993   S. Silverman

The author suggested that students will boost academic learning from games and so-called "play" activities. The case for doing something physical every day is growing. (From Journal of Educational Research.*)*

1994   P. Strick & F. Middleton

The authors showed that two areas of the brain that were associated solely with control of muscle movement, the basal ganglia and the cerebellum, are also important in coordinating thought. (From Science.*)*

1995   S. Brink

The author says there is tremendous value in novel motor stimulation throughout secondary school and the rest of our lives. (From U.S. News & World Report.*)*

1995   W. T. Thatch Jr.

Nearly 80 studies were mentioned that suggest strong links between the cerebellum and memory, spatial perception, language, attention, emotion, nonverbal cues, and even decision making. (From What Is the Specific Role of the Cerebellum in Cognition?*)*

1995   S. Greenfield

He has had spectacular success with autistic and brain-damaged children by using intense sensory integration therapy. Over the years, many teachers who integrated productive "play" into their curriculum have found that the learning comes easier. (From Journey to the Centers of the Mind.*)*

1996   S. Richardson

He was one of the first to make the link between the neodentate (only found in humans) and the significant role in thinking. One of his patients had cerebellar damage and, surprisingly, impaired cognitive function. Linking movement and learning became inseparable. (From Discover Magazine.*)*

1996   T. Dobie

In an aeronautics simulator study, Dobie found that repeated exposure to active bodily spinning and rotation significantly improved normal walking and other motor performance over days of practice. (From the National Biodynamics Laboratory.)

1996   W. Calvin

He states our brain creates movements by sending a deluge of nerve impulses to either the muscles or the larynx. Novel movements shift focus in the brain and engage the prefrontal cortex and the rear two thirds of the frontal lobes—the area of the brain often used for problem solving, planning, and sequencing new things to learn and do. (From How Brains Think.*)*

1996   R. Kotulak

There may be a link between violence and lack of movement. Infants deprived of stimulation from touch and physical activities may not develop the movement-pleasure link in the brain. (From Chicago Tribune.*)*

1996   J. Pollatschek & F. Hagen

They say, "Children engaged in daily physical education show superior motor fitness, academic performance and attitude toward school as compared to their counterparts who do not participate in daily physical education." (From International Health, Racquet, and Sportsclub Association Booklet.*)*

1996   P. Kearney

In Redcliffe Elementary School (Aiken, SC), test scores were among the lowest 25% in their district. After a strong arts curriculum was added, the school soared to the top 5% in six years. (From Star Tribune.*)*

1997	H. Kinoshita

He and fellow colleagues discovered that exercise triggers the release of BDNF, or brain-derived neurotrophic factor. This natural substance enhances cognition by boosting the ability of neurons to communicate with each other. (From BrainWork.*)*

1997	N. Weinberger

He says, "Arts education facilitates language development, enhances creativity, boosts reading readiness, helps social development, general intellectual achievement and fosters positive attitudes towards school." (From Music and Science Information Computer Archive Newsletter III.*)*

1998	J. Kesslak, V. Patrick, J. So, C. Cotman, & F. Gomez-Pinilla

Sedentary tasks are cognitively enhanced when combined with intermittent periods of stretching. Their recent study suggests that physical activity aids the sedentary body and learning brain by producing increased levels of a neuro-stimulator known as brain-derived neurotrophic factor (BDNF), which promotes neuron survival and growth, in addition to protecting neurons against deterioration. (From Behavioral Neuroscience.*)*

1998	J. Raber

His research points out the detrimental effects of chronic overproduction of stress hormones, from obesity to memory deficits. Chronic stress induces dendritic atrophy in hippocampal neurons, which are paralleled by cognitive deficits. (From Molecular Neurobiology.*)*

1998	L. Kilander, H. Nyman, M. Boberg, L. Hansson, & H. Lithell

The findings from this study add support to possibilities of intervention, such as exercise, in early stages in cognitive decline. (From Hypertension.*)*

1999	H. van Praag, G. Kempermann, & F. H. Gage

The authors conducted animal studies that suggest running and other aerobic activity promote brain cell regeneration and growth. (From Nature Neuroscience.*)*

1999	H. van Praag, B. R. Christie, T. J. Sejnowski, & F. H. Gage

Exercise makes mice smarter, Salk scientist demonstrates. The study shows that physical exercise triggers chemical changes in the brain that spur learning—at least in mice. Associated work suggests that similar mechanisms may operate in humans as well. (From Proceedings of the National Academy of Science USA.*)*

2000	B. J. Anderson, D. N. Rapp, D. H. Baek, D. P. McCloskey, P. S. Coburn-Litvak, & J. K. Robinson

Voluntarily exercising rats ran on running wheels attached to their cage for seven weeks and took 30% fewer trials to acquire criterion performance in a maze than sedentary controls. (From Physiology and Behavior.*)*

2001	California Department of Education

The study matched scores from the spring 2001 administration of Stanford 9 Test (SAT-9) with results of the same 954,000 students' performance on the state-mandated 2001 physical fitness test and found that students' academic achievement is related to their levels of health-related physical fitness. (From www.cde.ca.gov.)

| 2002 | H. van Praag, A. F. Schinder, B. R. Christie, N. Toni, T. D. Palmer, & F. H. Gage |

The authors demonstrated that newly generated cells mature into functional neurons in the adult mammalian brain. (From Nature.*)*

2003   R. E. Rhodes

Exercise increases hippocampal neurogenesis to high levels in mice bred for increased voluntary wheel running. The hippocampus is important for the acquisition of new memories. It is also one of the few regions in the adult mammalian brain that can generate new nerve cells. (From British Journal of Social Psychology.*)*

2003   S. Vaynman, Z. Ying, & F. Gomez-Pinilla

*Their results illustrate a basic mechanism through which **exercise** may promote synaptic-plasticity in the adult brain; a brain area whose function, learning and memory, depends on this capability. (From* Neuroscience.*)*

2003   J. S. Rhodes, H. van Praag, S. Jeffrey, I. Girard, G. S. Mitchell, T. Garland Jr., & F. H. Gage

This study suggests that neural growth in the hippocampus is increased as a result of high levels in mice bred for increased voluntary wheel running. The hippocampus is important for acquiring new memories and generating new nerve cells. This is the first evidence that neurogenesis can occur without learning enhancement. The authors propose an alternative function of neurogenesis in the control of motor behavior. (From Behavioral Neuroscience.*)*

2003   L. Lu, G. Bao, H. Chen, P. Xia, X. Fan, J. Zhang, G. Pei, & L. Ma

This study was designed to investigate the effects of social environments and play on learning and memory, neurogenesis, and neuroplasticity. The findings demonstrated that social environments and play can modify neurogenesis and synaptic plasticity in adult hippocampal regions, which is associated with alterations in spatial learning and memory. (From Experimental Neurology.*)*

2003   J. Brown, C. M. Cooper-Kuhn, G. Kempermann, H. van Praag, J. Winkler, F. H. Gage, & H. G. Kuhn

The authors discovered that an enriched environment and physical activity stimulate cell growth in the hippocampus. (From European Journal of Neuroscience.*)*

2003   A. J. Zametkin, C. K. Zoon, H. W. Klein, & S. Munson

Researchers performed computerized and manual searches of the literature and summarized the most relevant articles. The results of the paper were that the growing epidemic of child and adolescent obesity deserves attention for its immediate mental health and long-term medical complications. (From Medical Science Sports Exercise.*)*

2004   P. A. Adlard, V. M. Perreau, C. Engesser-Cesar, & C. W. Cotman

The authors found that, in rats, the cognitive benefits of exercise significantly increase over time. (From Neuroscience Letters.*)*

2004   G. S. Griesbach, D. A. Hovda, R. Molteni, A. Wu, & F. Gomez-Pinilla

The authors found that, in rats, voluntary exercise can help recover function after traumatic brain injury. (From Neuroscience.*)*

| 2004 | B. Will, R. Galani, C. Kelche, & M. R. Rosenzweig |

The authors corroborated earlier findings from animal studies that environmental enrichment and physical exercise increase neurogenesis in the hippocampus. (From Progress in Neurobiology.*)*

| 2004 | R. Molteni, A. Wu, S. Vaynman, Z. Ying, R. J. Barnard, & F. Gomez-Pinilla |

The authors unveiled a possible molecular mechanism by which lifestyle interacts with the brain. Exercise reverses the harmful cognitive effects of a high-fat diet on brain plasticity in animals. (From Neuroscience.*)*

| 2004 | C. Schmidt-Hieber, P. Jonas, & J. Bischofberger |

Neural stem cells in various regions of the vertebrate brain continuously generate neurons throughout life. Thousands of new granule cells are produced per day, with the exact number depending on environmental conditions and physical exercise. Newly generated neurons express unique mechanisms to facilitate synaptic plasticity, which may be important for the formation of new memories. (From Nature.*)*

| 2004 | P. A. Adlard & C. W. Cotman |

The authors identified voluntary exercise as an intervention that can reverse central nervous system dysfunctions such as cognitive decline, depression, and stress. (From Neuroscience.*)*

| 2004 | S. Vaynman, Z. Ying, & F. Gomez-Pinilla |

The authors found that exercise enhances learning and memory in animals. (From Neuroscience.*)*

| 2004 | J. C. Quindry, W. L. Stone, J. King, & C. E. Broeder |

This study investigated acute exercise and its effects of intensity and energy expenditure. It was found that intensity of exercise plays a huge role in postexercise stress while total exercise energy expenditure does not. (From Medical Science Sports Exercise.*)*

| 2005 | A. Das, D. Rai, M. Dikshit, G. Palit, & C. Nath |

This study researched the effect of acute, chronic-predictable, and chronic-unpredictable stress on memory. The rats were subjected to three types of stressors—(1) acute immobilization stress, (2) chronic-predictable stress, that is, immobilization daily for five consecutive days, and (3) chronic-unpredictable stress that included reversal of light/dark cycle. Conclusion: Chronic stress is very damaging to the brain. (From Life Sciences.*)*

| 2005 | A. A. Russo-Neustadt & M. J. Chen |

The authors studied brain-derived neurotrophic factor and antidepressant activity and the impact exercise has on depression. (From Current Pharmaceutical Design.*)*

| 2005 | N. Uysal, K. Tugyan, B. M. Kayatekin, O. Acikgoz, H. A. Bagriyanik, S. Gonenc, D. Ozdemir, I. Aksu, A. Topcu, & I. Semin |

The authors studied the effects of regular aerobic exercise in the adolescent period on hippocampal neuron density, apoptosis, and spatial memory. The study examined the effects of regular aerobic exercise on spatial memory and showed that exercise induced significant cognitive improvement throughout brain maturation in rats. (From Neuroscience Letters.*)*

| 2005 | A. S. Naylor, A. I. Persson, P. S. Eriksson, I. H. Jonsdottir, & T. Thorlin |

Running for an extended length of time inhibits exercise-induced adult hippocampal growth in the spontaneously hypertensive rat. Here it was reported that long-term running for 24 days results in a downregulation of hippocampal progenitor proliferation to one-half the level of non-running controls compared with a fivefold increase in progenitor proliferation seen after 9 days of voluntary running (short-term running). (From Journal of Neurophysiology.*)*

| 2005 | A. B. Niculescu |

Genomic studies of mood disorders—the brain as a muscle? The effects of exercise on mood suggest a superficial analogy and perhaps a deeper relationship between muscle and brain functioning. (From Genome Biology.*)*

| 2006 | A. Bjørnebekk, A. A. Mathé, & S. Brené |

Physical activity has documented beneficial effect in treatment of depression. It was found that antidepressant-like effect of running in an animal model of depression. (From Neuropsychopharmacology.*)*

| 2006 | E. T. Ang, G. S. Dawe, P. T. Wong, S. Moochhala, & Y. K. Ng |

The study was designed to examine the effects of 12 weeks of forced treadmill running on learning and memory performance in rats. The results indicate that forced exercise could influence learning and memory. (From Brain Research.*)*

| 2006 | S. Vaynman & F. Gomez-Pinilla |

Say no to sitting! This study looked at how lifestyle impacts neuronal and cognitive health through molecular systems. Exercise, a behavior that is inherently associated with energy metabolism, impacts the molecular systems important for synaptic plasticity and learning and memory. In the 21st century, we are confronted by the ever-increasing incidence of metabolic disorders in both the adult and child populations. The ability of exercise and diet to impact systems that promote cell survival and plasticity may be applicable for combating the deleterious effects of disease and aging on brain health and cognition. (From Journal of Neuroscience Research.*)*

| 2006 | T. Y. Pang, N. C. Stam, J. Nithianantharajah, M. L. Howard, & A. J. Hannan |

The authors suggested the differential effects of voluntary physical exercise on behavior. (From Neuroscience.*)*

| 2007 | D. M. Castelli, C. H. Hillman, S. M. Buck, & H. E. Erwin |

This study examined 259 public school students in third and fifth grades and found that field tests of physical fitness were positively related to academic achievement. (From Journal of Sports Exercise Psychology.*)*

| 2007 | A. Broocks, U. Ahrendt, & M. Sommer |

The authors studied physical training in the treatment of depressive disorders. Solid evidence has emerged that regular exercise is associated with therapeutic effects in psychiatric patients suffering from depressive and possibly other psychiatric disorders. (From Psychiatrische Praxis.*)*

| 2007 | Z. Radak, S. Kumagai, A. W. Taylor, H. Naito, & S. Goto |

The authors studied the effects of exercise on brain function: especially the role of free radicals. (From Applied Physiology, Nutrition and Metabolism.*)*

2007	J. G. Hunsberger, S. S. Newton, A. H. Bennett, C. H. Duman, D. S. Russell, S. R. Salton, & R. S. Duman

Exercise has many health benefits, including antidepressant actions in depressed human subjects, but the mechanisms underlying these effects have not been elucidated. This study looked into vascular growth factor (VGF) and its effect on depression. (From Nature Medicine.*)*

2007	J. L. Trejo, M. V. Llorens-Martín, & I. Torres-Alemán

The authors recognized the effects of exercise on spatial learning and anxiety-like behavior, including improved cognition and reduced anxiety. (From Molecular and Cellular Neurosciences.*)*

2007	C. W. Cotman, N. C. Berchtold, & L. A. Christie

This study supported findings that exercise builds brain health. The benefits of exercise have been best defined for learning and memory, protection from neurodegeneration, and alleviation of depression. Thus, through regulation of growth factors and reduction of peripheral and central risk factors, exercise ensures successful brain function. (From Trends in Neuroscience.*)*

2007	S. Brené, A. Bjørnebekk, E. Aberg, A. A. Mathé, L. Olson, & M. Werme

This study suggests running is rewarding and acts as a natural antidepressant. Natural behaviors such as eating, drinking, reproduction, and exercise activate brain reward pathways, and consequently the individual engages in these behaviors to receive the reward. (From Physiology & Behavior.*)*

2007	C. Engesser-Cesar, A. J. Anderson, & C. W. Cotman

The authors studied wheel running and antidepressant treatment. They have differential effects in the hippocampus and the spinal cord. (From Neuroscience.*)*

2007	M. Ploughman, Z. Attwood, N. White, J. J. Doré, & D. Corbett

Endurance exercise facilitates relearning of forelimb motor skill after a stroke. Exercise improves attention and learning, both critical components of stroke rehabilitation. (From European Journal of Neuroscience.*)*

2007	H. van Praag, M. J. Lucero, G. W. Yeo, K. Stecker, N. Heivand, C. Zhao, E. Yip, M. Afanador, H. Schroeter, J. Hammerstone, & F. H. Gage

This study recognizes that diet and exercise have a profound impact on brain function. In particular, natural nutrients found in plants may influence neuronal survival and plasticity. (From Journal of Neuroscience.*)*

2007	K. Van der Borght, R. Havekes, T. Bos, B. J. Eggen, & E. A. Van der Zee

Enhanced physical activity is associated with improvements in cognitive function in rodents as well as in humans. The authors examined in detail which aspects of learning and memory are influenced by exercise. The authors show that 14 days of wheel running promotes memory acquisition, memory retention, and reversal learning. (From Behavioral Neuroscience.*)*

2007	C. X. Luo, J. Jiang, Q. G. Zhou, X. J. Zhu, W. Wang, Z. J. Zhang, X. Han, & D. Y. Zhu

This study recognized voluntary exercise could improve the impaired spatial memory in stroke patients. (From Journal of Neuroscience Research.*)*

2007	H. Kim, S. H. Lee, S. S. Kim, J. H. Yoo, & C. J. Kim

Maternal exercise during pregnancy has been suggested to exert the beneficial effects on the brain functions of offspring. This could be a very important finding for the secondary level of at-risk students who become pregnant at a very early age. (From International Journal of Developmental Neuroscience.*)*

2007	R. M. O'Callaghan, R. Ohle, & A. M. Kelly

Exercise may have the potential to improve cognitive function. Here it was exhibited that forced treadmill-running results in selective improvements in hippocampal growth. Rats that underwent exercise training demonstrated enhanced expression of long-term potentiation in dentate gyrus and enhanced object recognition learning. Spatial learning in the Morris water maze was unaffected by exercise. These changes were associated with an increase in expression of brain-derived neurotrophic factor in the dentate gyrus. (From Behavioral Brain Research.*)*

2008	S. M. Buck, C. H. Hillman, & D. M. Castelli

The researchers investigated the relation between aerobic fitness and interference control—one component of executive control—in 74 children between 7 and 12 years of age. The findings suggest that increased levels of fitness may be beneficial to cognition during preadolescent development. (From Medical Science Sports Exercise.*)*

2008	J. J. Broman-Fulks & K. M. Storey

These authors conducted an evaluation of a brief aerobic exercise intervention for high-anxiety sensitivity. (From Anxiety Stress Coping.*)*

2008	J. L. Trejo, M. V. Llorens-Martín, & I. Torres-Alemán

The authors recognized the effects of exercise on spatial learning and anxiety-like behavior. (From Molecular and Cellular Neurosciences.*)*

2008	G. Chytrova, Z. Ying, & F. Gomez-Pinilla

Exercise normalizes levels of growth inhibitors after brain trauma. (From European Journal of Neuroscience.*)*

2008	C. H. Duman, L. Schlesinger, D. S. Russell, & R. S. Duman

Voluntary exercise produces antidepressant and anxiolytic behavioral effects in mice. Chronic wheel-running exercise in mice results in antidepressant-like behavioral changes that may involve a brain-derived neurotrophic factor (BDNF)-related mechanism similar to that hypothesized for antidepressant drug treatment. (From Brain Research.*)*

2008	S. W. Tang, E. Chu, T. Hui, D. Helmeste, & C. Law

The effect of short-term exercise (15-minute step-exercise) on serum brain-derived neurotrophic factor (BDNF) levels was evaluated in healthy human subjects. The result of this study supports the need for larger sample size in studies on BDNF changes in psychiatric disorders or psychiatric drug effects. (From Neuroscience Letters.*)*

2008	C. H. Hillman, K. I. Erickson, & A. F. Kramer

An emerging body of multidisciplinary literature has documented the beneficial influence of physical activity engendered through aerobic exercise on selective aspects of brain function. A growing number of studies support the idea that physical exercise is a lifestyle factor that might lead to increased physical and mental health throughout life. (From Nature Reviews Neuroscience.*)*

LET'S WRAP IT UP

The brain is a complex organ in which sensory, cognitive, and motor skills interconnect. It is important that instruction not try to separate brain functions into specific right- or left-brained tasks, but instead build an environment that stimulates and engages the whole brain. The brain has several systems, including pleasure/reward, fine and gross motor movement, balance, vision, sensory-motor, cognitive, memory, social/emotional, and attentional and alarm systems.

Verbal memory is not as strong as visual, emotional, and kinesthetic memory. Because individuals attend to and remember more of what they say and do than what they read and listen too, the bulk of classroom time should be spent engaging in activities that involve the senses and the whole body. Demonstrations, active movement and discussion, simulating, and hands-on tasks should be a preferred medium for delivering content and concepts and not just reserved for extension activities and classroom filler.

The mind-boggling facts emerging from current trends in the field of neuroscience as it relates to education are enough to get your heart pumping and your adrenaline levels elevated. One would have to be deserted on an island or living in a cave to not have noticed the impact science is having on how we really learn. Now that we have explored some amazing specifics, let's take a closer look at what the research says. With the conclusive evidence out, educators have a wealth of information with regard to the brain-body and reasons as to why they should energize their teaching.

3

Generating Energy and Maintaining Attention

People rarely succeed unless they have fun in what they are doing.

—Dale Carnegie

LET'S BEGIN

According to *Merriam-Webster's New Collegiate Dictionary*, *to energize* means "to give energy to; rouse into activity; be in operation; put forth energy." Sounds fun to me! Kids are wired to move. To incarcerate them to a chair for seven hours a day is crazy. How many times have you been to a lecture, a class, or a seminar where you were bored stiff? The energy level on a scale of 1 to 10 was about 2. You had no clue what the speaker was talking about as you were sorting out in your mind the grocery shopping list, plans with your significant other for the upcoming weekend, or all of the things you need to get done while you are wasting your time not listening to this speaker. Energizers to the rescue! Right when you think the zzz's are coming on . . . voilà! It's time to rock-and-roll to some movement.

CHECK THIS OUT

Oh yes, Las Vegas, Nevada, where on a mild summer day the temperature can reach a balmy 125°F. That's a bit toasty! At Lincoln Elementary School, the school year is in session until June 18, and then the kids are off to summer vacation. Lincoln Elementary offers summer school, which just so happens to be a big hit for this community.

Mr. Chadwick teaches summer school every year at Lincoln. He loves teaching and can use the extra money. Mr. Chadwick has come to the realization that "in teaching, you surely aren't going to get rich monetarily, but you will in many other ways."

Summer school is a tough assignment. Keeping the students on task and focused on the content is pretty much an act of Congress. They are thinking about all sorts of fun summer activities, and school is not one of them. In Las Vegas, cool pools are at the top of the list; it is very difficult for students to concentrate when they are hot and tired.

Mr. Chadwick, a sixth-year teacher, is very familiar with the impact of energizers and attention grabbers in academic classrooms, especially when his students start "zoning out." He knows that he has to "switch gears" and "states" to keep these kids tuned into the lesson. Approximately every 10 to 15 minutes, Mr. Chadwick will plan for something, even the smallest activity such as standing up, walking five steps in any direction, and saying "hi" to the closest person. After that, Mr. Chadwick will have the students share to at least one person around them about what the class was just reading in the text. This accomplishes a few positive objectives: (1) the students get an attention break, (2) the topic in the text is reinforced by students repeating and reviewing what they just read, and (3) the activity is fun.

Not only do the students need attention grabbers or breaks, but so do teachers. Mr. Chadwick decided at the next faculty meeting he was going to share with fellow teachers some essays and answers from some test papers that were submitted by his students. Yes indeed, humor is a great attention grabber and can be the much needed relief for the many stressed out, overworked teachers out there.

Here are some real gems:

- The body consists of three parts—the brainium, the borax and the abominable cavity. The brainium contains the brain, the borax contains the heart and lungs, and the abominable cavity contains the bowels, of which there are five—a, e, i, o, and u.
- Three kinds of blood vessels are arteries, vanes and caterpillars.
- Blood flows down one leg and up the other.
- When you breathe, you inspire. When you do not breathe, you expire.
- The skeleton is what is left after the insides have been taken out and the outsides have been taken off. The purpose of the skeleton is something to hitch meat to.

- H_3O is hot water, and CO_3 is cold water.
- The moon is a planet just like the earth, only it is even deader.
- Artificial insemination is when the farmer does it to the cow instead of the bull.
- Dew is formed on leaves when the sun shines down on them and makes them perspire.
- To prevent contraception: wear a condominium.

Surely many a smile was provoked from these essay answers by many a teacher. Oh, how many of us teachers have silly, fun, stories to share about our own classrooms and the creative minds of our students. So, the next faculty meeting you go to, compile a list or share Mr. Chadwick's list. The rest of the staff will be thrilled as you will have their attention to set a positive environment and maybe redirect any negatives that were scheduled on the meeting's agenda. Good luck!

WHY EVEN BOTHER?

Your students have just returned from lunch and their eyes are glazing over. Don't despair—energize them! The icebreakers and energizers in this section of the book can be used at any point during any type of lesson in your academic classroom. The benefits are countless when your students are shutting down and turning off their attention. Read on for some great ideas.

Energizers

Each energizer is accompanied by an energizer descriptor, what stuff you will need, and how to do it. They're short, quick, and sometimes physical, somewhat active—and always fun!

Use energizers to:

- *Promote readiness for learning*. Students do not learn well when they have low energy. Sluggishness can lead to a lack of attentiveness, and the phenomenon can be contagious with a class. Slouching in chairs, leaning on desks, and other nonverbal behaviors can be subliminally observed and copied by other class members. Energizers get students ready to engage in the lesson.
- *Create excitement*. You're excited about the content of your lesson. That does not mean that your students are equally stimulated. Learning is exciting to some children, but others sometimes seem not to want the experience. Energizers can generate a positive expectation of upcoming events.
- *Overcome the effects of fatigue, drowsiness, and drag*. Long days, hot rooms, difficult material—all these can put students in a kind of mild stupor. Energizers can "wake them up" to go on with the class refreshed.

- *Develop a sense of shared fun.* You can facilitate even the most serious delib- erations with comic relief, as long as you keep a proper perspective on the state standards and the outcomes of the lesson. An occasional group laugh can make any lesson more lively.

Sample energizing activities include the following:

- Celebrations—festive accomplishments
- Round of applause—creating a clapping circle in front of body
- Pen roll—flipping pen from "thumbs up" to a "thumbs down" rotation
- Wow—making "w's" with fingers on both sides of a wide-open mouth
- Standing "O"—standing up making a big "O" out of arms

The sample activities in Figure 3.1 are not "throw-ins" randomly inserted into the classroom. They are purposeful, and they need to be used strategically. Using energizers can greatly enhance the impact of learning at three specific times:

1. Just after a meal

2. After recess

3. When a long lesson begins to drag

These are the most common times when students are likely to be "de- energized," or less than optimally ready to go on with the class agenda. The pur- pose of using energizers is to focus the learner in the lesson and to raise the energy level of the class!

Enough already . . . let's get energized!

Figure 3.1   Quickie Examples

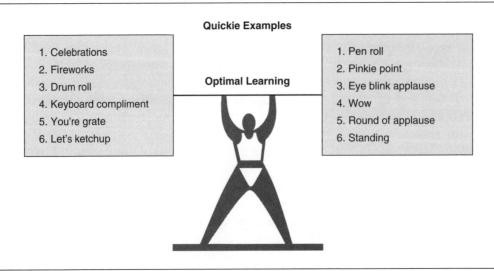

Quickie Examples

	Optimal Learning	
1. Celebrations		1. Pen roll
2. Fireworks		2. Pinkie point
3. Drum roll		3. Eye blink applause
4. Keyboard compliment		4. Wow
5. You're grate		5. Round of applause
6. Let's ketchup		6. Standing

READY, SET, ACTION!

ARTIST AND CANVAS

What Stuff Do We Need? Nothing

What Do We Do?

- Partner up group
- One person is the artist; one person is the canvas
- Artist creates a statue out of canvas
- All artists then go for a "gallery walk" looking at all statues
- Switch . . . artists now canvas, canvas now artists
- Repeat

DATA PROCESSING

What Stuff Do We Need? Nothing

What Do We Do?

- Line up participants by different criteria without talking (for example, height, years teaching, length of hair, etc.)

DANCING IN GELATIN

What Stuff Do We Need? Nothing

What Do We Do?

- Move in slow motion
- Mirror the movements of a friend in slow motion
- Switch leader/follower

PARTNER MACARENA

What Stuff Do We Need? Nothing

What Do We Do?

- Review single Macarena
- Partnered to music

THIRTY-ONE DAYS ON KNUCKLES

What Stuff Do We Need? Nothing

What Do We Do?

- Start by counting on index finger knuckle
- Then crevice next to it
- Next knuckle, next crevice, etc.
- In crevices, months ending on the 30th
- On top of knuckles, months ending on the 31st

HAND JIVE

What Stuff Do We Need? Nothing

What Do We Do?

- Clap two times on thighs
- Clap two times with hands
- Scissors four counts

- Fist two times, other two times
- Hitchhike two times, switch

FREEZE FRAME

What Stuff Do We Need? Nothing

What Do We Do?

- Do the twist song

- Freeze into bizarre position

ONE BEHIND

What Stuff Do We Need? Nothing

What Do We Do?

- Leader performs movement A (hands on hips)
- Players memorize it
- Leader performs movement B (hands on shoulders)

- Players perform movement A
- Players one movement behind
- All locomotor, nonlocomotor, and fitness movements are okay

CHAIR DANCE

What Stuff Do We Need? Chairs

What Do We Do?

- Students sit in chairs
- Perform movements to music while sitting

- Create cross-lateral patterns
- Be crazy!

PAPER PLATE DANCE

What Stuff Do We Need? Paper plates

What Do We Do?

- Two paper plates per person
- Rub plates together
- Wave plates

- Toss plates
- Whatever you want!

BALL TOSS

What Stuff Do We Need? Balls

What Do We Do?

- Toss ball to ask questions
- Toss ball to answer questions
- Create throwing patterns with balls

I LIKE PEOPLE WHO

What Stuff Do We Need? Nothing

What Do We Do?

- Instructor says, "I like people who" do . . . whatever
- Students act out what might be suggested

HAVE YOU EVER?

What Stuff Do We Need? Nothing

What Do We Do?

- Students are grouped in circle formation
- One student is in middle and asks, "Have you ever?" . . . whatever
- The "whatever" may be something like "gone to Hawaii" or "ran a marathon"
- The students who can answer yes to a question switch places
- Middle person moves to outside circle in an open slot
- Whoever is left out is now new middle person who asks questions

DOG AND BONE (ON TABLE)

What Stuff Do We Need? Wadded paper ball

What Do We Do?

- Put paper ball on table
- Have students group up in fours
- Students are a 1, 2, 3, or 4
- Two teams of four compete against each other
- When teacher calls out one of the numbers, that number grabs for ball

NO HANDS

What Stuff Do We Need? Various objects

What Do We Do?

- Use different objects
- Can't pick it up with hands
- Students move to various locations in room

LIMBO TRAIN

What Stuff Do We Need? Long jump ropes or poles

What Do We Do?

- Two students are holding rope or pole tightly
- The rope/pole should be slanted so students have a choice of how "low they can go"

- Repeat by going through multiple times to fun music

CLAPPING GAMES

What Stuff Do We Need? Nothing

What Do We Do?

- Create clapping patterns
- Connect patterns to create new games

- Kids love this!

PENNIES PASS

What Stuff Do We Need? Pennies

What Do We Do?

- Line students up in groups of six facing each other
- At the "go" signal, students pass a penny from one player to another on team

- Each team tries to "fake out" the other team
- At "stop" signal, each team tries to figure out where the other team's penny is

LAP SIT IN CIRCLE

What Stuff Do We Need? Nothing

What Do We Do?

- Put group in circle formation
- All face clockwise

- Then sit on laps of person behind
- Switch, facing counterclockwise

SWITCH SOMETHING GAME

What Stuff Do We Need? Nothing

What Do We Do?

- Partner up, facing each other
- Both partners turn around, changing three things about themselves

- Face each other again, trying to figure out what is changed

1–20

What Stuff Do We Need? Nothing

What Do We Do?

- Group up with about six people
- Stand shoulder to shoulder in tight circle
- Heads facing down, each player says a number (i.e., one, then two, and so on)
- If two players says a number at the same time, start over

PSYCHIC SHAKE

What Stuff Do We Need? Nothing

What Do We Do? Students pick a number in their head … either 1, 2, or 3. It's a secret! When the music starts, students are to handshake each other the number in their head without saying or lip synching the number. If a student has the secret number 1 and shakes hands with a student who shakes three times, the student with secret number 1 knows to continue on and look for someone who shakes only once. The class should end up in three groups, the 1's, the 2's, and the 3's. Fun activity.

AURA

What Stuff Do We Need? Nothing

What Do We Do? Students stand facing their partners at arms' length. They touch palms and close their eyes. Keeping their eyes closed, partners drop their hands and both turn around in place three times. Without opening eyes, partners try to relocate their energy bodies by touching palms again. Very fun and contagious.

SHOULDER CIRCLES AND MASSAGE

What Stuff Do We Need? Nothing

What Do We Do? Entire class gets into one big circle. Students put their hands on the shoulders of the person in front of them. Students massage back. Then circles on one right side of back, circles on left side of the back, then figure 8's. (This is excellent for brain stimulation.) Next, doodles (back and forth with both hands) from top of back to bottom. Let the students know they are exercising their brains . . . they love it!

POWER WALK

What Stuff Do We Need? Stopwatch

What Do We Do? Power walking or race walking is a great way to increase the heart rate for a longer period of time. Challenge your students to see if they can walk as fast as you can! This is a very fun activity with heart rate monitors. The students are very surprised that their heart rate increases so much just from walking! Try partner power walking.

JUGGLING

What Stuff Do We Need? Juggling scarves

What Do We Do? Each student gets three scarves, two scarves are put in their waistband and one scarf is in their hand. To the music, toss the scarf up, catch it on top (so knuckles are facing up). Next, two scarf juggling with both hands. Cross, drop, catch them on top. When this is mastered, criss-cross, applesauce. Students should say this out loud. Next, two scarf juggling with one hand. Demonstrate proper holding technique. Hold one scarf against palm with middle finger, ring finger, and index finger. The other scarf goes between thumb and index finger of same hand. Put hand you are not using behind your back. Practice with one hand, then the other. Next, three scarf juggling with both hands. Demonstrate proper holding technique for students. Put two scarves in one hand (as previously explained) and one scarf in the other. The first scarf to be thrown is the scarf held with the thumb and the index finger, in the hand that is holding two scarves. Before it begins to fall, toss the scarf, in the hand holding only one scarf, across the other way. So you are making an X across your body. After you throw the second scarf, your hand comes down to catch the first scarf on top. Then you toss the third scarf (the one held against your palm with three fingers) across your body and then that hand comes down to catch the second scarf on top. Yippee!!!

CRISS-CROSSIES

What Stuff Do We Need? Nothing

What Do We Do? Also called hookups, this is another super-great brain activator and perfect as a closing activity. While standing, students cross legs, cross one arm across the other clasping their hands with fingers interlocked, turn clasped hands under toward their chest (a hookup), put tongue on roof of mouth, and breathe deeply. It's incredibly relaxing. This activates many parts of the brain because of the many crossovers across the midline of the body. The tongue on the roof of the mouth adds another dimension to brain stimulation.

BALLOONS BONANZA

What Stuff Do We Need? Balloons

What Do We Do?

- Tap-kick-knees-feet with balloons
- Over-under head and legs
- String on ankle
- Balloon sit
- Wwhhhhffffff balloon races
- Balloon walk

- Balloon balances
- Balloon across midline
- Balloon and elbows
- Balloon elbow pass
- Balloon knee pass

SUPER-QUICKIE AWESOME ENERGIZERS

What Stuff Do We Need? Nothing

What Do We Do?

- Laughter is the best medicine . . . tell jokes
- Line or circle dancing
- Add-ons with words or sentences
- Back rubs in circle formation; switch directions
- Back to back standup/stretches
- Circle run-ons
- Eye scream
- Chicken dance

- Three crazy faces (back to back and match faces)
- Beach ball where fingers touch
- Scavenger hunt with words and definitions
- Shower curtains for movement
- Clapping rhythms
- Stories in a circle
- Count to 10

- Creative handshakes
- YMCA
- Expert interviews
- Duck, duck, goose (more movement variations)
- Psychic faces
- Instant replay
- Thumb wrestling
- Keep away
- Lap sit
- Mill mill (say cues)
- Commercial breaks
- Musical chairs (all win)
- One up, One down
- The rest of the story . . .
- Order circles (height, birthdays)
- Pass the face/sound
- Toe-tac-tic . . . you want opponent to win
- Poster potpourri

- Questions in a circle
- Room change
- Simon says (with traps)
- Stretch and breathe
- Tea party (snob, jock, nerd, etc.)
- Movement for the masses
- Truth/truth/lie
- Word of the day
- Yes clap!
- Clap once, clap twice
- Birdie song
- Cross laterals
- Good news/bad news
- Silly rules time
- Serious rules time
- Wiggle waddle relay
- Tongue twisters

These energizers are basically self-explanatory. If you're not sure what to do, make up your own "rules" to the energizer. The main objective here is to motivate and invigorate the learning process through movement.

State Changers

When learning new material, students are bombarded with masses of sensory data. Throughout all of the uploading of this new information, somehow the learning goals must stand out in the student's mind. State changes are an effective technique for highlighting what needs to be of focus. A state change can be something that brings about a change in a student's thoughts, feelings, or physiology (Allen, 2001). Combining repetition and state changes increases recall and comprehension.

Teachers have already learned to deal with attention issues when planning instruction. Employing methods such as alternating repetitive sedentary activities with pleasurable, active activities are successful because interest and enjoyment can overturn a depressed attentional system. Sylwester and Cho (1993) point out that instructional methods such as math relay games are not directly related to math, but "artificially engender attention-getting excitement through rapid action," taking advantage of the students' stable attentional mechanisms. Our brain's attentional system is set up to prefer high contrast, originality, and exciting connotations (see Figure 3.2).

In many ways, attention and motivation are inherently linked. An individual who is motivated to attend will more likely activate brain processes that allow for assimilation of new information. Hickey (2003) notes that the actual act of participating in a knowledgeable activity changes knowledge and meaning, much in the way that internalization of social processes are dependent on participation in those social processes.

Figure 3.2   Attention Grabbers

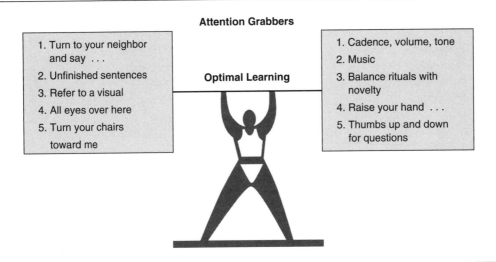

In so much as learning and constructing meaning are influenced by the individual's motivation and participation in the learning process, it must be recognized that each individual comprehends and participates in a distinctive way. To prepare learners to approach content from a brain-based perspective, teachers should incorporate active instruction into the classroom.

As a kid, how long can you pay attention? What factors influence your attention span? A good indicator of time would be about 10 to 15 minutes. Attention may be for longer periods, depending on several factors:

- The time of day
- The child's interest level in the topic
- The energy and expertise of the instructor
- How the child is feeling
- How well the child's basic needs have been met
- How comfortable the child is in the group
- What happened to the child before coming to class

Research indicates that after about 10 minutes, 20 at the most, attention will begin to wander. State changes are ideal to keep the attention of the learner.

The good news is that state changes do not have to be complex, expensive, or lengthy to be effective! At the end of this section of state changes is a simple list of quick ideas to grab the attention of your learners. Have fun!

GROUP STATE CHANGERS

What Stuff Do We Need? Nothing

What Do We Do?

- Pair share 1-2-4-8
- Assign 1-2-3-4 at a table (all #1 discuss)
- Change tables, change seats
- Create discussion groups
- Mingle, mingle, mingle (and then point according to teacher cues)
- Turn to your group and discuss
- Rumps up
- Sit creatively
- To add to with info
- Group changes position
- Team cheers

DIRECTIONAL STATE CHANGERS

What Stuff Do We Need? Nothing

What Do We Do?
The following—just say:

- Turn to your neighbor and say . . .
- Raise your hand if . . .
- Refer to a visual
- All eyes over here
- Turn your chairs toward me
- Thumbs up and down for questions
- Take a deep breath . . . if you agree, let it out
- If you're ready to learn, please do . . .
- Turn to your team leader and say, "Let's do it!"
- Find at least one person near you and say, "Yes!"

TRAVELING STATE CHANGERS

What Stuff Do We Need? Nothing

What Do We Do?

The following—just say:

- Find a new seat
- Take seven steps
- Red, green, yellow (stop, go, get ready)
- Move to another location
- Touch two walls
- Touch something green, blue, etc.
- Crawl under and over
- Meet three people who
- Change location

QUESTION STATE CHANGERS

What Stuff Do We Need? Nothing

What Do We Do?

The following—just question, "Who is?"

- Good lookin' as
- Smart as
- Same color shoes as
- Same middle initial as
- Same sport as
- Brilliant as
- Same size shoe as
- Same color eyes as
- Same birthday month as
- Living closest to

BASIC STATE CHANGERS

What Stuff Do We Need? Nothing

What Do We Do?

Just do:

- Balance rituals with novelty
- Unfinished sentences
- Voice: Cadence, volume, tone
- Music: Cadence, volume, tone

GREAT IDEAS STATE CHANGERS

What Stuff Do We Need? Depends on idea

What Do We Do?

Just do it:

- Jokes
- Cartoons
- Musical chairs (noneliminating)
- Pen twist
- Hand puppets
- Eraser exchange
- Twisted arm
- Carpet sharks
- Pinkie point
- Cross-laterals

TOSSING OBJECTS STATE CHANGERS

What Stuff Do We Need? Depends on idea

What Do We Do?

Just do it:

- Tossing out candy
- Tossing a pen in the air
- Tossing papers
- Tossing a ball/balls
- Tossing, spinning, and catching

("Tossing Objects State Changers" is from Jensen, 2003)

MUSIC AND MOVEMENT

There are overwhelming reasons why it makes sense to add some music into teaching. It's easy and fun! Whenever you as the instructor have the opportunity to "liven-up learning" with some music, please do! Children respond positively no matter their language, gender, or age.

When using music for transitioning, remember to have very clear start and stop cues. This will eliminate any unnecessary problems as the children are very clear that (1) when the music is playing they move and (2) to stop when the music stops. A remote is a must for quick transitions.

Enjoy! I am confident that with a little practice, you will agree that your students are more engaged in the lesson with added music.

MAKE IT HAPPEN

An attention grabber is a wonderful technique to start a class or to energize any given moment. If done properly, these active team strategies create an enhanced learning environment, boost the team's work, and get students acquainted, talking, and involved.

Some instructors love to start with icebreakers, while others want to dive right into the content of the class. When you do decide to do your activities, follow these guidelines for success:

- *Make it quick*—Especially the first few times you do a team activity, make sure it lasts no more than five minutes; ideally, you would like to break the monotony of "lecture only" by doing more of them. If your class meets for more than an hour, you can increase the time accordingly.
- *Involve everyone*—Make sure the activity has everyone actively involved. This means no wallflowers—everyone has something to do or is expected to contribute in some way. If in a very large group, create smaller teams or breakout groups that allow everyone to interact and participate in the activity or movement-based discussion.
- *Make it okay to pass*—For whatever reason, some people may not want to participate. In the introduction, tell your classmates they can say "pass" if they don't want to participate.
- *Be relevant*—Most kids will go along with the activity if it has some relevance to the team's work. Introduce the icebreaker, why you chose that activity, and what the benefits are, especially if the activity is a game or is unusual.
- *Be appropriate*—Select an activity that will work with your class's preferences and styles, education level, and background.
- *Keep it simple*—Many teams in classrooms start out with a pure and simple activity. As the team matures, you may try more personal or elaborate procedures.
- *Be prepared*—Practice the activity in advance with your family or friends to make sure you understand the guidelines. Bring instructions, handouts, or supplies with you and set up the space appropriately. When it's time, transition into a crisp explanation of the rules. (It's always a nice touch to post the key rules on an easel chart for all to see.) Make sure everyone understands the rules and processes before you allow them to begin.
- *Be flexible*—Adapt the activity to meet the needs of your class. Even though you have prepared yourself with a "dry run," the activity may not go as planned. That's okay; go with it! There's always a learning point; even if the activity is an utter failure in your eyes, debrief the activity in a very real and genuine way. You and your class will learn from the mistake.
- *Keep it lively*—After the class has done a few easy icebreakers, try a different type of activity. There are dozen of books on icebreakers, warm-ups, team activities, and games that may inspire you to try something different. If you want to encourage flexibility of mind, look for imaginative and creative activities.

- *Enjoy yourself*—If you are looking forward to the warm-up, then others will too. Keep a sense of humor and don't take side comments too personally.
- *Debrief the activity*—Take a moment to apply the activity to the team's work. Ask the team, "What happened? What did you learn? How does it relate to the team's work? What's next or is there something we need to do?"
- *Thank them*—At the conclusion of the activity, thank everyone for participating and continue with the lesson plan.

After a while, the class will expect these activities, and you can experiment with the length, content, and different methods. Encourage other classmates to bring in new class activities and to build the team. You'll find that classmates learn from each other what they like and dislike, what works and what doesn't, and how they work together as individuals and as a team.

LET'S WRAP IT UP

The journey you are taking by adding "attention grabbers" and "music" into your teaching is meant to change your instruction forever. The days of endless daydreams and mindless duties will hopefully be minimized. Will they diminish all daydreaming and zoning out? Absolutely not; however, there will be a dramatic decrease in this behavior.

Have fun with the process! Don't be hard on yourself and feel overwhelmed. One step at a time. Keep in mind that you've already taken the most important step toward livening up learning. You are reading *Action-Packed Classrooms* and ready to implement its powerful tools. Let's move on.

4

Integrating Movement and Academics

A teacher is one who makes himself progressively unnecessary.

—Thomas Carruthers

LET'S BEGIN

Aligning movement and academic concepts are essential for true learning to occur. The integration of content-area information with movement can often be accomplished with minimal effort and maximum benefit. The benefit to students is twofold; they increase their learning of physical activities and academic knowledge as well as recognize the interconnectedness between physical activity and how it applies to all areas of their lives. Learning is anchored through procedural learning; the act of doing instead of watching increases students' learning of the content exponentially. So, set down that pencil, stand up, and let's do learning.

CHECK THIS OUT

When it comes to teaching first grade, Mr. Miller is as qualified and successful as they come. Although he has been teaching for only two years, you wouldn't know it. His demeanor, rapport, and communication skills with children are phenomenal.

Teaching at Oakville Elementary School in Columbus, Ohio, is a treat in itself. The school is brand-new and is located in a very safe area. Mr. Miller has had some ups and downs as a beginning teacher. On the upside, he's a great teacher! On the downside, his success has created tension and slight jealousy with some of the veteran teachers on staff.

Why would some teachers be threatened by a "pipsqueak" new teacher such as Mr. Miller? Because this guy is doing all of these fun, creative, engaging activities inside his classroom . . . unspeakable! The kids love his class. During lunch one day, one of the teachers was overheard in the faculty lounge saying, "We'll just see what happens when the state testing scores come in. I'm sure this nonsense will stop then! Then he'll really have to start teaching like he should be."

But little did they realize that Mr. Miller was well-read, up-to-speed, and knowledgeable about how children learn. His motto was, "The outcome is for my students to *learn*, not for me to teach." The focus needs to be on the outcome. And indeed, his students did learn. Not only did his state scores come back top at his school, but top in the district as well.

Reflect on this scenario. Have you as an educator seen the likes of this at your school? Are your teachers keeping up-to-date with what the research says about how we as humans really learn? Is your staff working cohesively in "firing up" the learning process at your school?

After celebrating his victorious scores on the state test, Mr. Miller collected old, well-known proverbs for his language arts class. He gave each kid in his class the first half of a proverb and had them come up with the rest. His intentions were to have the children turn these proverbs into "action proverbs" by adding movement with music. Of course, the assignment was delayed, as Mr. Miller was caught off guard with the hilarious results from this assignment, some of which are listed below. Enjoy!

- As you shall make your bed, so shall you . . . mess it up.
- Better to be safe than . . . punch a fifth grader.
- Strike while the . . . bug is close.
- It's always darkest before . . . daylight savings time.
- Never underestimate the power of . . . termites.
- You can lead a horse to water but . . . how?
- Don't bite the hand that . . . looks dirty.
- No news is . . . impossible.
- A miss is as good as a . . . mister.
- You can't teach an old dog new . . . math.
- If you lie down with the dogs, you'll . . . stink in the morning.
- Love all, trust . . . me.
- An idle mind is . . . the best way to relax.
- Where there's smoke, there's . . . pollution.
- Happy the bride who . . . gets all the presents!
- A penny saved is . . . not much.

- Two's company, three's . . . the Musketeers.
- Don't put off tomorrow what . . . you put on to go to bed.
- None are so blind as . . . Helen Keller.
- Children should be seen and not . . . spanked or grounded.
- If at first you don't succeed . . . get new batteries.
- You get out of something what you . . . see pictured on the box.
- When the blind leadeth the blind . . . get out of the way.
- There is no fool like . . . Aunt Eddie.

Just when you think you've seen or heard it all from your students, there's always room for a few more laughs.

Your decision to read on, grab these great energized academic classroom ideas, and take your teaching to a new active level will reap many rewards. Not only will your students embrace the love of learning, but you will truly have so much more fun.

WHY EVEN BOTHER?

"Why bother?" is comparable to the question "Why put gas in a car?" Because it works! Learning academic subject matter through different modalities will only reinforce the content in multiple mediums. The hierarchy of learning explains this well.

The Learning Hierarchy

In a traditional classroom, the usual routine is children read, they hear what the teacher has to say, and they see what is on the board. Of what we see and hear, half of the content has been retained, and learning has occurred. As you climb the learning pyramid (see Figure 4.1), you can see that the more engaged the learner, the more learning occurs. Ninety-five percent of what is actively being taught is retained. Works for me!

Instructional methods should offer high contrast, alternating between repetitive sedentary activities and active lessons. Instruction should take a cue from media and include more visually stimulating, interactive material. Instruction should be diverse. Students need to be taught that there are learning preferences and differences in the way the brain receives, processes, and expresses information.

Subjects that traditionally and solely use linguistically based content instruction should try to incorporate more movement, music, and action into their instruction. Learning programs for children with attention deficit disorder and with learning and mental disabilities should incorporate movement into classroom instruction. Body-centered learning that incorporates energizers, attention grabbers, and aerobic recess/physical education should be routinely included in instruction. Stimulating, engaging instruction should be given increased priority in the school day, and active exercises should also be incorporated into other areas of classroom instruction.

Figure 4.1 The Hierarchy of Learning

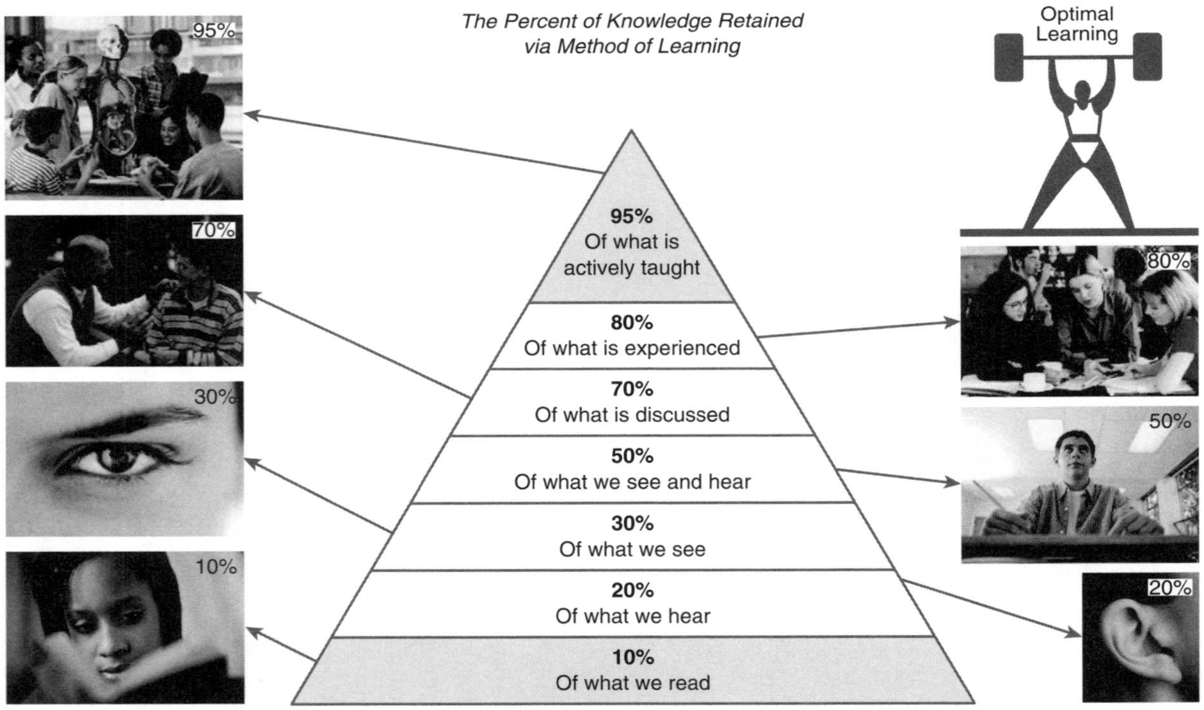

The Percent of Knowledge Retained via Method of Learning

Optimal Learning

95%
Of what is actively taught

80%
Of what is experienced

70%
Of what is discussed

50%
Of what we see and hear

30%
Of what we see

20%
Of what we hear

10%
Of what we read

95%

70%

30%

10%

80%

50%

20%

Figure 4.2   Integrating the Concepts of Movement With Educational Subject Matter

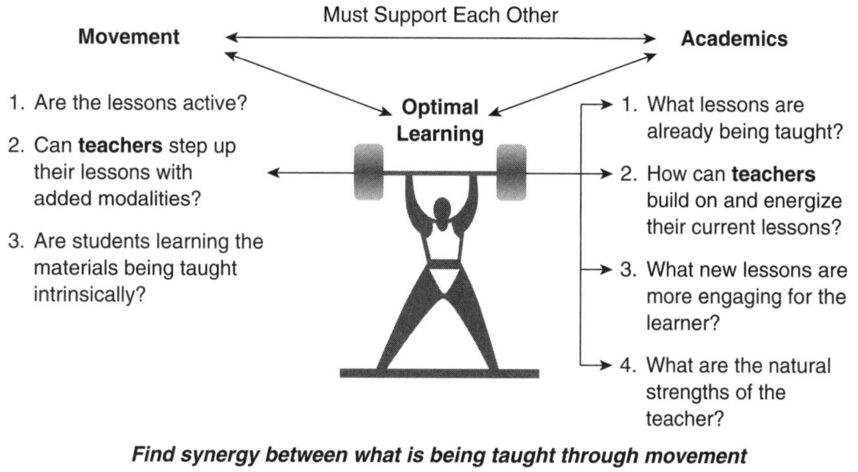

Find synergy between what is being taught through movement

Anchoring Learning

Figure 4.2 poses critical questions that teachers should ask when planning their lessons. These questions need to be thought of carefully as more movement is added to the curriculum:

- What are you teaching?
- Who are you teaching?
- Are they learning the material being taught?

When adding more action, teachers do not need to reinvent the wheel. Most teachers have a wealth of information and tools that they are already using. The questions for teachers should include "How can I step it up a notch?" or "What can I add to what I am already doing?" Taking your strengths and building on them only makes sense. You're good at what you do—just add to it.

Academic Movement Reminders

The following activities in the pages to come provide much needed action in math, language arts, science, social studies, and health/physical education. There are a few reminders about the activities before proceeding:

Age-Level Specification

Because of the varied abilities and uniqueness of each student, the activities are geared for most grade levels. You will have to be the judge of that as you peruse these academic reinforcers, asking yourself, "Will this work with my kids?" Take the activity of "phonics phitness," for example. Phonics has to do with early elementary material, and you may be teaching upper elementary. However, the game can be a template for more mature kids if you take the basic guidelines and adjust them to the material you are teaching. Don't throw out an idea before doing a little investigating first. It just may be your students' new favorite game.

Equipment Issues

Because most of teachers out there in "teacherland" don't have equipment, the activities are flexible enough to use whatever works. Instead of poly spots, paper plates have been substituted. Of course, if you have poly spots, use them!

Safety Issues

When substituting such things as paper plates versus poly spots, safety is of utmost importance. Paper plates slide on the ground as opposed to poly spots, which are sticky. When moving around with plates on the ground, be careful the kids stand by them and don't land on them. As for other homemade equipment or substitutions, think safety first.

Creativity

Do what works for you. There may be a game or an activity that you may need to tweak to make it happen with your kids. Do whatever it takes to make learning come alive for you, and don't be afraid to add your one-of-a-kind touch to it.

Facilities

Every school is different. Some schools have big classrooms; team teach so one room is roomier; have indoor multipurpose rooms, gymnasiums, or wonderful outside playing areas. Adapt. If there is a will, there is a way.

Activity Descriptors

The activities cut to the chase because teachers do not have time to read through a ton of stuff to do an activity. So, the advice is, just do it. The main objective is to get your students engaged in active learning. If the activity doesn't go perfectly, no problem. The kids won't notice; they're just happy they get to move.

Music

Whenever possible, include music. Music is a very powerful hook into any activity as it just makes it more fun. In many subject-matter activities, there is music that is a subject-matter match for the activity. Do whatever you can to reinforce the academia. The game descriptors do not tell you to use music and a boombox when figuring out "what stuff do we need?" Ask yourself, "What music could I use here?"

Now, it's time to get 'em moving. Enjoy.

ACTION-PACKED MATHEMATICS

HUNDREDS CHART

Why Are We Doing This? To reinforce mental math strategies

What Stuff Do We Need? Hundreds chart (available through Fit4Learning; visit www.Fit4Learning.com for more information)

How Do We Play? Each student has a hundreds chart while sitting in his or her seat. Teacher cues students to put finger on correct number on hundreds chart by calling out cues; for example, "Put your finger on the number of sides in a triangle, double it, square it." After several cues, around 10, the students raise their hands, and each one is on a certain number. Once the teacher reveals the answers, she says, "Change tables, change seats." At that time, really cool music is playing and the kids can move to any spot they want to in the room. When the music stops, students are ready for next set of cues.

MATH MAYHEM

Why Are We Doing This? To learn to solve simple math computations

What Stuff Do We Need? Groups of four; one pair of throwing dice

How Do We Play? Have one person in each group throw one die as specified (underhand, overhand, dominant hand, nondominant hand, etc.). Each member in the group will have to form the number thrown with their body. Do this a few times and alternate throwers and use high, medium, and low levels. Variety can be added by making the numbers with just the legs, arms, left side of body, or right side of body.

Now get with a new group of four and throw the pair of dice as specified above in different ways. If the teacher tells the students to add, the students must add the numbers thrown and make the answer with their body.

To add some variety, the students can throw the dice, get the answer (whether by adding or subtracting, etc.) and can, for example, hop the answer (i.e., $6 + 2 = 8$ hops or $4 - 2 = 2$ jumping jacks).

In addition, one group can visit another group, and the one group makes the problem with their bodies and the other group has to answer the problem. Subtraction, multiplication, and division can be used.

OLYMPIC MATH

Why Are We Doing This? To reinforce order of operations in math

What Stuff Do We Need? Pencils, worksheets, throwing dice, and playing cards

How Do We Play? Have each student find a partner. Each partnered-up group gets a deck of cards and a pair of throwing dice along with their pencils/paper. The cards are mixed up, and 16 cards are dealt on the table faceup in a four-row, four-column setup.

One student rolls a die. Whatever the number, that is the "answer" he or she tries to reach. For example, if a six and three are rolled, that would be added up to nine. The object of the game is to combine cards by adding, subtracting, multiplying, or dividing until you reach the number nine. Jacks, queens, and kings are counted as tens; aces are counted as ones. The maximum number of cards a player can combine is five in one round. Players take turns. When there are no more cards on the table, add up the values of the cards; whoever has the highest number wins that round. Continue with deck.

In addition, when the dice are rolled, the numbers on dice can be multiplied together for a larger number for the older kids.

JUMPIN' & HOPPIN' HOOPS

Why Are We Doing This? To reinforce math skills

What Stuff Do We Need? Hula hoops and foam dice

How Do We Play? For a small class, spread out 6 to 10 hula hoops so that they are all touching (creating a web of hoops). If the class is large, set up two to three sets of webs, so that the groups of students remain between four and six at each web of hoops. Have student roll the dice and add or subtract the two numbers.

The children then determine if the number is odd or even. If the number is an odd number, they hop through the hoops on one foot. If the number is an even number, they jump through the hoops on two feet. Example: 4 + 1 = 5, an odd number; they hop five times in and out of all the hoops as fast as they can.

The teacher can vary the locomotor skill by using galloping for odd numbers and skipping for even numbers.

MULTIPLES IN MOTION

Why Are We Doing This? To learn multiples of the numbers one through nine

What Stuff Do We Need? Balls/paper wads/objects of different sizes, shapes, and weight

How Do We Play? The teacher begins by giving an example for multiples of one and two by doing the following: Multiples of one: one clap. The students (led by the teacher) count by ones and clap their hands together for each number up to nine. Multiples of two: one clap and one snap. The students (led by the teacher) clap their hands and then snap their fingers. They count by twos when they snap (up to 18). Example: "Clap," "Snap (two)," "Clap," "Snap (four)," "Clap," "Snap (six)," etc.

Next, the students are arranged in groups of three or four, and a number is assigned to each group using the numbers three through nine. Each group must come up with a clapping/snapping/stomping pattern for the multiples of their number. Multiples of three must have three sounds (e.g., stomp, clap, snap), multiples of four must have four sounds, five must have five sounds, etc. The students are given approximately 15 minutes to get their patterns together.

The students are to design a similar sequence using throwing, catching, kicking, or dribbling. Each person in the group can do a single part of the sequence, or each student can do the complete pattern. (For example, for two times two, the students might bounce the ball twice and throw the ball twice.) They are free to choose from a variety of balls of different sizes, shapes, and weights. Finally, each group will present both of their "Moving Multiples" to the class.

JUMPING NUMBERS

Why Are We Doing This? To practice addition and subtraction skills

What Stuff Do We Need? Lots of open space, one jump rope for each student

How Do We Play? Each student will get a jump rope and get into his or her personal space. The teacher will then call out various math problems appropriate to the grade level.

The students will call out the answer to the problem and then jump the rope the number of times that equals the answer (counting out loud). The teacher will vary the jumping skill by asking students to jump forward, backward, while crossing the rope, while moving, or in other ways that have been taught previously in the class.

HUMAN NUMBER LINE

Why Are We Doing This? To recognize a number line

What Stuff Do We Need? Paper numbers (or numbers on index cards) −12 to +12 for students' use, large set of numbers (or index cards) −12 to +12 for teacher's use, four cones/objects

How Do We Play? Begin class by explaining the number line. Have a large picture of one on the wall. Explain the number order. Have students line up on a line, arms length apart. Have two teams doing this facing each other. At the end of each line have a cone/object. Explain to the students that they are standing in a number line. They are one gigantic number line!

Give them each a paper number or index card (one team has red numbers/index cards and one team has blue numbers/index cards) in the correct order so that when you give them out, students will be standing in the proper order for a number line. Now give them each a poly spot if you have them. This represents their spot on the number line.

Start with numbers 1 through 12. When the music starts, children will move around in a manner told (walk, gallop, etc.). When the music stops, they will return to their team in the correct number order, with their number held above their head to show they are finished. The team to complete this first scores a point.

The next task is to ask them to make numbers with their bodies. When you hold up a number, the teams must go to their area and form that number with their bodies in a standing position. The whole group must work together to make one number. When you see that the number is made, you will then call out "number line." At that time, both teams must hustle to get back in number-line order.

Points are awarded for the team that makes the number first and the team that gets back in order first. If you make the number 8, you get 8 points. If you get back in number-line order first, you get half that amount of points, or 4. Students are asked to keep their scores as a team. They must add the numbers each round. The teacher will prompt for the answer, "You had 7 points, you made the number 3 first, so what is your score? You also got back in number-line order first, so now what is your score (add half of 3)."

RECIPES FOR SUCCESS

Why Are We Doing This? To apply math skills to real life

What Stuff Do We Need? Copies of recipes, pictures of the ingredients, price sheets of all the groceries, jump ropes, pencils, one sheet of paper to multiply and divide, desk or table, pencil, calculator, yummy surprise

How Do We Play? The stations need to be set up to include the following:

- The recipe box
- The grocery store
- The checkout lane
- The kitchen
- The bakery manager's office

Do the following:

- Students are paired with a classmate. Each pair begins in the recipe box and selects a recipe
- Students run to the grocery store and shop for all the items in their recipe
- Students jump to the checkout lane and add up all their groceries
- Students skip to the kitchen and work at a station

At each station, there is a single jump rope, a pencil, a division sheet, and a multiplication sheet.

- Students divide the recipe in half while the partner is jumping rope
- Students switch when completed
- Students multiply the recipe by two while the partner is jumping rope and switch when completed

When finished in the kitchen, students take their work to their manager for work approval. While the manager is checking their work, they run around the "circuit" (the playing area).

PLACE VALUE TAGGERS

Why Are We Doing This? To learn place value of numbers to the millionths place

What Stuff Do We Need? Jerseys/colored buttons/whatever to identify taggers, index cards with various numbers up to the millionths place

How Do We Play? Scatter children in the area with three quarters of kids as taggers and one quarter kids as card holders. On the musical signal, children move using different locomotor skills as directed by the teacher (skip, jog, leap, hop, jump) and try to tag or avoid the tag. Tagged children freeze in a "number" statue.

To move again, a place value card holder must come to them, and they have to answer the question. For example, if the place value card has the number 196 on it and the "1" is circled, they need to say what place value it is worth. If correct, they move, if not, the person needs to help them figure it out. Change taggers and card holders every minute to keep the game fresh.

MEASURING UP

Why Are We Doing This? To work on estimation skills

What Stuff Do We Need? One rope, hoop, yardstick, pencil, and paper per child

How Do We Play? Before starting the class, review math concepts of inches, feet, and yards. Give each student a rope to place in his or her personal space. Make sure the rope is pulled tight and in a straight line. Have students start at the end of their rope and use their feet to measure the length in approximate feet. If a student "falls off," have him or her begin again.

Ask the students to compare the length of the rope to the length of the hoop in feet and to eventually find a hoop in the class that matches the length of their rope. Students will also be given a yardstick to determine how close in actual feet their "feet" are to the actual measurement on a yardstick. As students are making measurements, request different ways to balance as they move up and down the rope; travel at a high level, crouching, backward, sideways, on two body parts, etc.

Fun challenges to ask the students:

- Can you walk four feet on your tightrope without falling off? Three feet backward? Five feet on a low level? How many times do you have to go up and down your rope to move 12 feet? How many feet long is your tightrope? Record your answer on your worksheet.
- Can you measure the number of feet in your hoop? How many feet are there in moving around your hoop three times at a medium level? Can you move six feet backward on your hoop? Is the number of feet in your hoop greater or less than the number of feet in your tightrope? Record answers on your worksheet.
- Get a yardstick and measure the actual number of feet on your tight rope. Is it the same size as your hoop? How can you get the actual measurement of the number of feet in your hoop? Record that number on your card. How many inches is the tightrope, the hoop? How many yards is the tightrope, the hoop?

Record your answers on the "Measuring Up Worksheet" (located in the Resources) and share with others.

CLOCKWISE CRAZINESS

Why Are We Doing This? To teach clockwise and counterclockwise direction

What Stuff Do We Need? Four cones/objects with signs, 12 paper plates/poly spots, cut numbers 1–12 (or numbers written on paper plates), a large cone/object and a small cone/object set on its side

How Do We Play? Have the students find a large space in the playing area. Introduce/review the concept of clockwise and counterclockwise with the class. Make a large clock to go in the center of the gym floor (in the jump-ball circle if in a gym) using numbered paper plates and cutout hands (or bats/yardstick/whatever) for the hands of the clock to give the students a point of reference. Place a sign with different movement skills on them in the corners of the gym (i.e., jog, skip, walk, grapevine, gallop, jump, leap).

Tell the students to begin moving clockwise using the skill that is on the sign closest to them. When the music stops, they will move to the opposite side of the playing area. Clockwise or counterclockwise will be called out as they are moving to the opposite playing side. When they reach the opposite playing side, begin the music and the students will begin moving in the direction specified using the skill on the card closest to them. Repeat as many times as necessary and vary the locomotor skills that are used (two- to three-minute song). If the students are confused, stand at the clock on the floor and walk around it in the correct direction specified.

Next have the students apply the math skills of addition and subtraction to the clock. The teacher will instruct the students to imagine what time they would like to be on the clock. Have the students make that number with their bodies or hold up the proper number of fingers. The teacher will then tell them they are to add two hours to the clock, so what time would it now be? Have the students do the locomotor movement that is closest to them, three times around the playing area (students might skip three times around the playing area in the direction specified). The teacher could follow the same approach with subtraction problems as well.

MATH CIRCUITS

Why Are We Doing This? To review basic math skills

What Stuff Do We Need? Really, anything you can get your hands on. For example, long/short jump ropes, beach balls, hula hoops, beanbags, lollipop paddles, Nerf tennis balls, Koosh balls, gator skin/foam balls, playground balls, yarn balls, foam bat, and index cards.

How Do We Play? Set up stations (you will need a fairly large area for this). The following is an example of how to set up stations; of course, it would vary with what kind of equipment you would use:

- Number of jumps over a rope
- Count to a number while hula hooping
- Throw beanbags into a target
- Volley balloons with lollipop paddles or body parts
- Toss balls at a target
- Toss ball underhand into trash can
- Number of soccer kicks to a wall (gator skin foam balls)
- Number of basketball dribbles
- Number of tosses and catches (Koosh or yarn balls)
- Hit beach balls off a tee/cone

Make index cards with math facts appropriate for your grade level (2 + 3 = ?, 7 × 3 = ?, 35 + 14 = ?). Have the cards at each station. The students draw the top card, solve the problem, and do that many skills at each station.

Assign two students at each station, allow them to complete the task and go to the next station. Go through the circuit as many times as possible. Adapt, modify, and add more or less stations as needed.

ACTION-PACKED LANGUAGE ARTS

POET AND DON'T KNOW IT

Why Are We Doing This? To reinforce spelling words and vocabulary

What Stuff Do We Need? Paper, pencil, colored markers, crayons, etc.

How Do We Play? After handing out paper and drawing/writing utensils, ask the students to write their first name vertically down the left-hand side of the piece of paper in front of them. Encourage them to use different colored markers and to be creative.

Have the students spell their names with their bodies, letter by letter.

Next, after moving to each letter and after having written them, students are to write a spelling or vocabulary word that has been covered in class at some point. They can use words that describe their feelings and thoughts about their class. They must have a word for each of the letters of their name. They are also allowed to draw things on the paper as well.

LOCO MOVES

Why Are We Doing This? To understand the differences between verbs and adverbs

What Stuff Do We Need? Index cards for each student with verbs on half the cards (i.e., skip, hop, slide) and adverbs on the other half (i.e., quietly, rapidly, quickly). One beanbag per student.

How Do We Play? The students should be in their own personal space throughout the general area. Spread the index cards throughout the playing area.

Prior to throwing, the teacher will give directions on various types of throws to use: that is, throwing underhand; overhand; on a low, medium, or high level; with the dominant or nondominant hand. The students will use the identified throw to throw their beanbags to a card and move as directed (backward, forward, sideways) to the card. Students should read the word on the card and decide if the word is a verb or an adverb.

With each person holding the card above his or her head, a student holding an adverb card will move to a student with a verb card. The pair will then perform the action on the cards (skip quickly).

Once all the students have performed the actions, place the cards back on the floor, pick up the beanbag, and move back into the personal space. Repeat the activity, this time finding a different verb/adverb.

WORD SHOOT OUT

Why Are We Doing This? To practice and reinforce spelling skills

What Stuff Do We Need? Six to eight basketball shooting stations, one basketball per station, poly spots/paper plates marked with letters, list of appropriate spelling words. Remember, modify regular balls and buckets if you don't have basketball courts.

How Do We Play? Students are split into groups of three. One student is designated to be the shooter, one the runner, and one the rebounder. Poly spots/plates are placed on the floor inside the basketball three-point line or the designated shooting area. The poly spots/plates are marked with a variety of letters that spell various spelling words.

The teacher calls out a spelling word. The shooter needs to spell the word by making shots from the proper letters. After a shot is made, the runner picks up the spot/plate with the appropriate letter on it and places it on the baseline in the proper order. The rebounder collects missed and made shots and passes the ball back to the shooter.

Once the group decides that they have spelled the word correctly, they sit on the floor (do toe-touch stretching) beside the letters to wait for the teacher to check the spelling. The group that successfully spells the word first gets to pick the next spelling word to use. The role of each person in the group rotates with each word (i.e., shooter to runner, runner to rebounder, rebounder to shooter). Students within the group should be encouraged to help the "shooter" and "runner" spell the word correctly by calling out letters in the word.

SCRABBLE SCRAMBLE

Why Are We Doing This? To work on increasing vocabulary knowledge

What Stuff Do We Need? Index cards with all the letters of the game Scrabble (i.e., 10 t's, 8 r's, etc.), scrap paper, and pencil for each group

How Do We Play? Divide the class into groups of two to three; any larger and the students will not receive the cardiovascular benefit. Spread all the cards (start with them faceup) on one half/quarter of the playing area.

- The students are in their groups equidistant from the cards and spread out in a safe manner.
- On the signal, students hop, jump, or skip one at a time to collect one card and bring it back to their partner or group.
- The students then try to form words from the letters they have brought back.
- The students must alternate their turns in getting letters. Once a word is formed, the students call the teacher over to verify that it is indeed a word (the teacher needs to place herself or himself in the same place equidistant from the groups, preferably on the outside of the groups and in the middle so students aren't running in front of others playing the game).
- If it is a word, then the students write down their word on their scrap piece of paper, gather up all their letters (they don't have to use all of them), and spread them back out on the floor at the other end of the playing area.

All words fewer than four letters score one point for each letter in the word. All words with five or more letters are worth two points for each letter. Total points for a class total.

BODY LANGUAGE

Why Are We Doing This? To encourage proper spelling and body depiction of two-letter words

What Stuff Do We Need? Lines on the playing area, paper and pencil for each group

How Do We Play? Before playing the game, discuss the word cooperation and how important it is to work together to complete the activity. The class is divided into groups of three students, and each group finds their personal space near a line on the floor. Give each group paper and a pencil, and have the students write down five two-letter words.

Using their bodies, students are to begin to form the letters to spell each of their five words. They must spell the word correctly, and the teacher must be able to be read the word from left to right on their "baseline." The teacher will move randomly around the room to read the words. After all five words have been spelled, students need to think of three-letter words to spell.

Each group tries to see how many words they can spell before the class is over. Have students spell the words with the entire body, the upper body only, the lower body only, the left side of the body, and the right side of the body. Change the students' position from crouching to a medium and then high level. This activity can be included with lessons on moving in different ranges and changing shapes.

PHONICS 4 PHITNESS

Why Are We Doing This? To teach phonics through movements

What Stuff Do We Need? Three sets of 26 paper plates/poly spots, with one letter written on each plate

How Do We Play? The teacher will scatter the three sets of plates/poly spots around the room and divide the class into small groups of three to four. The teacher should call out a series of questions concerning phonics along with a basic locomotor skill. The children are to perform the skill as they move to answer the question (based on what the students have already learned).

Make students aware that there are several sets of each letter. For example, "Hop to the letter that makes the "huhh" sound like in the word "house." The teacher should try to use each letter at least once.

ALPHABET TAG

Why Are We Doing This? To work on letter recognition

What Stuff Do We Need? Cones to mark off a safe playing area

How Do We Play? Have the students spread out safely in the playing area. Identify two-thirds of students as "taggers." When taggers tag someone, that person must freeze immediately and then make a letter with his or her body. To unfreeze a frozen person, a free runner must come up to him or her and must correctly guess the letter that classmate has made.

Students are not allowed to make a letter that has them lay on the floor. Illegal letters are "X," "T," "I," and "L." Taggers aren't allowed to tag classmates during the guessing process.

SENTENCE DETECTIVES

Why Are We Doing This? To recognize the parts of a sentence

What Stuff Do We Need? Index cards with different nouns, verbs, and adjectives on them to put together to make complete sentences. The verbs should be action words that the students can do as a group (i.e., twist, jump, bend). Create enough words so that sentences can easily be formed.

How Do We Play? Set out the index cards, randomly, facedown in a specified area within the playing area (on one end, side, or in the middle of the playing area). Form small groups of two to three students and have each group find their own personal space, which will be on the opposite side of the playing area from the index cards. They need to be equidistant away from the index cards. You may want to put a cone/object next to each group to mark where they are supposed to be.

On the teacher's signal, one student from each team will walk, crabwalk, hop, or whatever locomotor skill the teacher specifies to the pile of index cards and choose one. Students will then return to their groups, tag the hand of the next teammate in line, and that teammate will proceed to the pile of index cards, using a specified locomotor skill, choose a card, and return to his or her group.

The group will continue this until they can make a complete sentence out of the chosen words. Once a completed sentence is made, the group should stand and call out "Word Play," at which time they are to do the action of the verb in their sentence. If more than one verb or noun is chosen, then the student who chose that card will hand it off to the next teammate in line; that teammate will return that card and choose another one. After a specified amount of time for each team to complete the sentence, the teacher will go around to each team and ask them to read their sentence out loud. The group will then be asked to recognize each part of the sentence—the verb, the noun, etc.

VOWEL SNATCHER

Why Are We Doing This? To work with and identify different vowel sounds

What Stuff Do We Need? Cones/objects to mark off a safe playing area, jump ropes, cones/objects or tape to mark lines at the end of the playing area

How Do We Play? Split class in half and have half of the students stand on a line at the end of the playing area. Have the other half stand on a line at the other side of the playing area. Assign each student a vowel. Identify two taggers (they can hold a small foam ball/object) to stand in the center of the playing area.

The teacher calls out a word. If a student's vowel is contained in that word, he or she tries to move across the room (skipping, sliding, galloping, walking, etc.) without being tagged. If the vowel runners get tagged, then they become taggers, so no one is eliminated. If the vowel runners cross the line on the other side without being tagged, they continue to be vowel runners.

You may want to have them write down the words they were during the activity. Have them identify the vowel and/or consonant in writing back in the classroom.

ABSOLUTELY ADVERBS

Why Are We Doing This? To reinforce the concept that adverbs describe the verb. The activity can be modified to reinforce the correct spellings of adverbs (adding an "ly").

What Stuff Do We Need? Background knowledge on adverbs and how they are written correctly

How Do We Play? Start by reminding the students that most adverbs end in -ly and that their most common use is describing verbs.

- Students move around the general space doing various movements.
- Students alter the way they are doing the skills by listening to the adverbs being called out by the teacher. For example, start with walking.
- Students walk at first and then add the adverb by telling them to walk quickly. Switch to walking slowly, nonchalantly, quietly, loudly, carefully, etc.
- Change the locomotor skills and alter the adverbs to those that best suit those new skills.

ACTION-PACKED SCIENCE

MOLECULES IN MOTION

Why Are We Doing This? To teach characteristics of molecules and the three states of matter

What Stuff Do We Need? Boundary markers

How Do We Play? Announce to the students that they are molecules, and molecules always move. They can move anyway they want, however, they can't touch one another.

Begin with a large area clearly marked by the cones that you set up.

- Have the students move for about one minute and stop. Decrease the area.
- Have the students move again. Repeat this in a very small area. Remind them not to touch each other. They are now in a small area and warmed up.
- Have them sit down and quickly explain that molecules that are far apart are gases (like the first time they moved). When the area was decreased, they were closer together. Molecules that are closer together are in a liquid state. When molecules are so close together they can hardly move, this is a solid.
- When the students are "liquid," they can "melt" or "ooze" at the end, and when they are "solids," they can "freeze" in a shape. This would reinforce the idea if the walls were enlarged step by step again after they were decreased.

THE CATERPILLAR SONG

Why Are We Doing This? To reinforce the changes of a butterfly

What Stuff Do We Need? None

How Do We Play?

- Sing verse one. Sing it again and have the class sing verse one with you. Sing verse two. Have the class sing verse two with you. Sing verse three. Have the class sing verse three with you.
- Demonstrate the motions for verse one. Have the class do the same. Demonstrate the motions for verse two. Have the class do the same. Demonstrate the motions for verse three. Have the class do the same.
- Sing the entire song with motions a few times through. Have the students do it once by themselves.

Song: three verses to the tune of "Mary Had a Little Lamb."

- First verse: "I'm a fuzzy caterpillar, caterpillar, caterpillar. I'm a fuzzy caterpillar about to make a cocoon."
- Second verse: "I'm wrapped in a cocoon, a cocoon, a cocoon. I'm wrapped in a cocoon about to spread my wings."
- Third verse: "I'm a pretty butterfly, butterfly, butterfly. I'm a pretty butterfly about to fly away."

Movements:

- First verse: Hold out your left arm, bending your elbow so your forearm is parallel to your chest. Use your right hand to imitate a caterpillar crawling along the ground (your left forearm).
- Second verse: Wrap your arms around yourself as if you were giving yourself a hug. Twist your torso right and left just to add more motion.
- Third verse: Spread your arms out to your sides and "flap" them up and down as if you are flying.

HABITAT HAPPENINGS

Why Are We Doing This? To learn how organisms interact in one habitat

What Stuff Do We Need? One mat for a dog house and a playground ball for the "dog" to play with, cones for a grasshopper's house, tennis balls to build an ant hill, an area for a human's home, jump ropes or something to form pathways for "worms" to travel

How Do We Play?

Procedure:

- Divide the class into groups of three.
- Each group is assigned an organism to act out (dog, grasshopper, ants, humans, worms).
- Have different stations with equipment for organisms to use while working in their lawns.
- Have stations randomly placed in area.

Activities:

- For now, organisms stay in their own areas. Allow students to experiment and work with equipment in the area that they are assigned for five minutes. Remind students to move the way and speed the organism does!
- Now use the same activity, but let students (courteously) take other organisms' equipment. Who will end up with the most equipment (the stronger, faster, larger organisms)? Tell students not to disrupt anything and to just take what is not being used.
- Again, same activity as above, this time no reservations. Every organism for itself! Remind students to act and move as the organism that they are does!

PLANET HOOP

Why Are We Doing This? To reinforce facts about each planet

What Stuff Do We Need? A hoop for each child, any children's books about planets. Use Gustav Holst's *The Planets* music while they are flying and fade it out when they are going to land.

How Do We Play? To begin this activity, each child needs a hoop. Have children stand in hoop holding it at medium height. Explain that we are going to take a spaceship trip to the planets. Children can move their body and hoop to low level for "blast off." Count backward from 5 to 0 and "blast off." Designate the specific movement pattern (walk, run, skip, hop gallop, leap) the child should execute while flying his or her craft in outer (general) space. Children can leave the hoops on the floor after blast off to make executing the movement pattern easier.

Have students land by placing hoop and body on the floor. The teacher will decide on a planet that they have landed on. When they land, use the books and pictures to tell them two or three facts about that planet. "Blast off" again.

Change the movement pattern, land on another planet, and talk about it, etc. After visiting four or five planets, return to Earth. Have children discuss how Earth is different from other planets.

PEDOMETER PROWLERS

Why Are We Doing This? To integrate plants/soil/rocks with movement

What Stuff Do We Need? Scavenger hunt paper (teacher-made depending on materials available), clipboard, and pencil for each group; pedometer for each student. If you don't have pedometers, no problem. Have students count steps and estimate.

How Do We Play?

- Introduce/instruct the students on the value of pedometers.
- Demonstrate how to use the pedometer and give the students some short practice time to experiment.
- Divide the students into small groups (four to five) and give each group a scavenger hunt worksheet. Students will use their knowledge of plants/rocks/soil to find items listed on the scavenger hunt worksheet.
- Review all of the items on the list that they are to find.
- Students are to use a different type of locomotor skill as they travel to each site. Record the skill that was used on the scavenger hunt worksheet.
- Discuss the boundaries for the hunt outside, if needed.
- When the list is complete, turn in the clipboard and wait for the other groups to finish.
- Once everyone has finished, move back inside and open up the pedometers. Ask students to write down the number of steps on the scavenger hunt worksheet.

Use this time to discuss:

- Place value.
- Estimation (estimate how many steps that they think they might take during the activity and then have them subtract the actual steps and estimated steps to find out the difference. Have they overestimated or underestimated?)
- Addition, subtraction, multiplication, and division.
- The ability to categorize the objects found (How are they classified?).
- Track or record steps taken (compare/contrast steps taken between/among activities).

PLANET CATCH

Why Are We Doing This? To reinforce the names of the planets, their order in relation to the sun, and the revolving of the planets around the sun

What Stuff Do We Need? A variety of different-sized balls for each child that will bounce, 10 cones of various sizes with the names of a planet on each cone

How Do We Play? The children will know the names of the planets by looking at the signs on the cones. Planets are assigned a number in relation to their order from the sun. For example, Mercury—1 bounce, Venus—2 bounces, and Pluto—9 bounces. The children will bounce the ball the number of specified times as the teacher calls out the planet. The teacher will count and bounce with them to reinforce the numbers. The teacher will also bounce the ball a specific number of times while the children watch and listen. The children will count and choose which planet corresponds to the number of bounces. This encourages children to use their auditory and visual skills.

Once children become familiar with the planets, the class will be divided into nine planet groups. The cone with the sun is located in the center of the gym. The planets are spread out in a line toward one side of the gym. Children are to line up behind their specified cone planet. Cone sizes can vary according to planet size—the smaller cones for the smallest planets and largest cones for the larger planets.

Teacher demonstration will show each group their orbit around the sun. On go, children will bounce and catch their ball around the sun, making their planets orbit. The children are encouraged to walk as they bounce and catch their ball as they "revolve" around the sun.

The following points can be stressed to the children:

- The difference in time it takes for the planets to make one orbit (Mercury will be walking in small circles while Pluto will be walking in a larger circle). Comparisons can be made; for example, Mars takes 88 days for one orbit, Earth takes 365 days, and Pluto takes 248 years.
- The rotation of planets as they orbit around the sun. Children can turn around as they move in their orbit to demonstrate planet rotation and why we have day and night.
- Differences in temperature in relationship to their distance from the sun. This activity can also be done with different locomotor skills and movements.

CREATURE FEATURE

Why Are We Doing This? To learn about ocean creatures

What Stuff Do We Need? Scooters (modify if necessary), ropes, mats, variety of balls

How Do We Play? Students should be in groups of three to four. Each group should be allowed to choose from the available equipment listed above to carry out the activity. Ask the students to recall an animal they learned about in the ocean unit taught in the classroom.

The students are to get the equipment necessary to demonstrate the movements and behaviors of these creatures as they travel throughout the playing area. An example would be students who study the rocky seashore would demonstrate the way a sea star moves and eats its prey. Give three students a scooter (or adaptation of some sort), and they must figure out how to make the star and move across the sea (gym) to their prey and capture and eat it.

After the students move, ask them to describe their movements. What type pathways were used? What directions did you travel in? Other examples could be octopus, sea lion, birds of the wetlands, crabs, and fish.

ENERGY CHASE

Why Are We Doing This? To teach how the blood flows and carries oxygen from the lungs to the heart and to the body (muscles) to create energy

What Stuff Do We Need? One flag belt (or sock) for each student with one (red) flag/sock, a bucket of extra red flags/socks, hula hoops, hurdles, cones, and noodles (tunnels for obstacle course of the heart), posterboard and markers for signs, cones for boundaries. (Modify and adapt whatever materials you have.)

How Do We Play?

Set up: The playing area should be set up with a large area for the tag game that represents "the body" and a smaller area (preferably a long thin area at the end of the game area) where an obstacle course can be set up that will represent "the heart and lungs."

To build the obstacle course (this is an example depending on what materials you use):

1. Build a tunnel with an arch (using hula hoops or noodles). Label with a blue sign that says, "Right Atrium—walk or crawl."
2. Tunnel labeled with a blue sign reading, "Tricuspid valve to the right ventricle—walk or crawl."
3. Tunnel labeled with a white sign reading, "To the lungs."
4. Place a bucket of extra flags in the lung area.
5. Hurdle labeled with a white sign reading, "Exit the lungs."
6. Hurdle labeled with a red sign reading, "Left atrium—jog or move fast."
7. Hurdle labeled with a red sign reading, "Bicuspid valve to the left ventricle—jog or move fast."
8. Hurdle labeled with a red sign reading, "To the body," with an arrow directing the traveling path to the tag playing area—"the body."

To play the game:

After explaining the flow of blood and how oxygen is carried from the heart and lungs to the muscles to create energy, you are ready to explain the game. All students who have on one belt and one red flag are "oxygenated blood." Choose four to six taggers to be "muscles" who have on a belt with no flag. At the start of the game, they are all "oxygenated blood" with one flag on their belt, moving through "the body" (the tag area).

The "muscles" try to take the oxygen from the blood (red flags) to create energy. If a "muscle" takes a player's oxygen (red flag), then the player becomes "deoxygenated blood" and must leave "the body" and travel though "the heart" (obstacle course) beginning at the right atrium, to the right ventricle, then to the lungs where he will pick up "oxygen" (one red flag) and re-flag himself. He is now oxygenated and can travel to the left atrium, left ventricle, and then to "the body" (tag area) and is back in the game.

Change "muscles" every two minutes. It is helpful to have a chart or poster diagram of the heart up on your wall in the playing area during your demonstration and explanation.

HOOP IT UP

Why Are We Doing This? To learn the bones in the human body

What Stuff Do We Need? Hula hoops, one for each student

How Do We Play? After instruction regarding the skeletal system and practice naming and labeling major bones in the body, the students will be challenged to twirl the hula hoops on the bones as called aloud by the teacher. This will require that the student remember the location of the bone and demonstrate the coordination required to successfully manipulate the hula hoop.

PULSE

Why Are We Doing This? To teach the effect of inactivity on a person's heart rate

What Stuff Do We Need? A clock, paper, pencil for each child, CD/tape player, and a variety of music that has different tempos (i.e., slow, relaxing music to lively, fast-paced tunes)

How Do We Play? After students enter the activity area, have students sit in their own personal space. Review with them how to take their own heart/pulse rate and then handout writing utensils and the handout. Have them take their pulse for 10 seconds as they are sitting in a resting position. Multiply that number by six, and then they need to record their resting heart rate on the paper. (Students can either work alone or in pairs to record their pulse rates on the paper.)

Have students put paper and pencil in a safe space on the side of the activity area. Then ask the students to walk around the general space for a while to the pace of some slow, soothing music. Then, have them stop to take their pulse and then record the results on the paper.

Next, have the students skip or jog around the general space to slightly more up-tempo music. Have them stop, take their pulse, and record the results on the paper. Then, have the students move in the space as fast as possible around the general space to very energetic, fast-paced music. After a few minutes, stop, take pulse, and record on paper.

Now it is time to reverse the process of the above explanation and begin to lower the pulse using slower-paced music. Each time use music that corresponds to the desired pace by first:

- Moving semiquickly (i.e., hopping, skipping, jogging) for a few minutes. Take pulse and record on the handout.
- Moving slowly (i.e., walking, strolling, etc.) through activity area. Stop, take pulse, and record on the handout.
- Sitting down and resting in personal space. Take pulse and record on the handout.

To close the lesson, discuss the results while seated. Why did we do this? What did this demonstrate? If you want you can have them compare their results with a friend or classmate.

DINO-SOAR

Why Are We Doing This? To reinforce concepts about dinosaurs

What Stuff Do We Need? Eight-inch gray soft PVC pipe wraps (two per tagger), 3-foot gray soft PVC pipe wraps (two per tagger), one set of 8-inch and 3-foot lengths for one tagger. Green and red Nerf balls (or other objects that are green and red). Modify PVC wraps with anything nonthreatening.

How Do We Play? Divide the class so that a student will be either a carnivore or herbivore and have only one omnivore.

- The carnivores will carry two 8-inch tubes close to their chest ("T-Rex").
- The herbivores will carry two 3-foot tubes using them on the floor like legs ("Stegosaurus").
- The one omnivore will have one of each of the tube lengths.
- Everyone else will carry either a green ball (plant food) or a red ball (meat). The carnivores can only tag the "meat" (red balls), herbivores can only tag the "plants" (green balls), and the omnivore can tag anyone.
- If tagged, the "meat" will lie down on their back (with feet in the air) and can be freed by another "meat" person who tags the "dead meat" on the feet.
- If tagged, the "plants" are frozen dead trees and can be freed by another "plant" person who tags the "dead tree" on the shoulder.
- After one minute, one quarter of the class changes to be a dinosaur, and the other students may switch being "plants" or "meat."

To close the lesson, discuss the activity. Review the content.

ACTION-PACKED SOCIAL STUDIES

CONFEDERATE GAME

Why Are We Doing This? To learn about Confederate states

What Stuff Do We Need? Paper plates and map of states on wall or overhead

How Do We Play? To play the game, follow these steps:

- States of Union and states of Confederacy written on plates
- Scatter in center of room
- Half of participants on one side; half on other side
- Object of game . . . to get all Confederates on one side

- All Union on the other side
- Get plates and take back to side (no peeking)
- Only one plate at a time
- Only one state per person

In conclusion, review and allow processing time of "what they just did."

CREATIVE CONTINENTS

Why Are We Doing This? To learn/review important facts about each of the continents

What Stuff Do We Need? "Fact cards" (blank index cards; remember that the fact must be unique to that continent so it does not confuse the students), a layout of each continent (easily made by drawing a simple outline of the continent), a variety of equipment that can be used for balancing such as ropes, poly spots/paper plates, beanbags, balls, carpet squares (whatever works for you)

How Do We Play? Prior to the activity the teacher will spread the layouts of the continents around the room and will lay a random stack of fact cards down in the middle of each continent layout.

- Students will be scattered around throughout the general space.
- The teacher will review the different types of equipment that are available for the students to use in their balancing skills.
- Give each student a "fact card." The teacher instructs the students that they are to use a different type of balancing activity as they travel to each continent.
- The students may balance beanbags on their heads, travel backward at a low level across the rope, step sideways on the individual poly spots, or dribble a ball across the rope as they move.
- The student reads his or her fact card and proceeds to use the given balancing skill to get to the appropriate continent.
- Once at the correct continent, the student will draw another fact card from the pile and once again move to the correct continent.
- Students will keep their fact cards throughout the game so they can use the cards to write down the fact and answer on a sheet of paper upon finishing the activity.
- Throughout the activity, the teacher will call out "balance switch," and the students must begin doing a new balancing skill.

The activity is over when the fact cards run out or when the teacher ends it.

CIVIL WAR DATES

Why Are We Doing This? To learn about time periods and major events during the Civil War; to reinforce the use of numbers

What Stuff Do We Need? Playing cards scattered in center of room facedown and an Internet Civil War date list of events from www.civilwar.com

How Do We Play? To play, follow the sequences below:

- Groups of six
- Specific date of event will be read, for example, April 19, 1861, was when President Lincoln set up a blockade

- Go get numbers to match date one card at a time
- No peeking at number until with group
- If not a good number, next person takes back

Once the group has all of the cards to make the numbers according to the date, the entire group shouts out "date mate." The teacher confirms and continues with another round and so on. The cards of each round are given to the teacher to mix in with other cards facedown.

PLAYING CARD DECK-CHECK

Why Are We Doing This? To provide students with an opportunity to enhance their knowledge about subject matter across the curriculum while engaging in a fun warm-up activity

What Stuff Do We Need? (1) One (or more if you wish) deck of playing cards, (2) two milk crates (or boxes), (3) four to eight sheets of paper set up around the playing area to indicate stations, (4) one sheet of paper set up as the "key," (5) Scotch tape, and (6) pencil/marker

How Do We Play? Make several photocopies of a U.S. map. On each map, highlight a different state. Along the bottom of the page write the name of the state, the state capital, and an activity. For example, "Sacramento, California. 15 pushups." "Albany, New York. 25 jumping jacks." Then tape the maps up around the gym. Tape up East Coast states on one wall, West Coast states on the opposing wall, etc.

Somewhere on the sidelines, place two milk crates next to each other. One will be upside down with the playing cards scattered faceup on it. Along the wall here tape the key. The key will tell the students which station to go to. "2 or 3—California," "4 or 5—New York," etc.

To begin the activity, assign your students to squads. Teachers should determine how many squads to have and how many students should be in each one based on the playing-area size.

When the teacher says "go," one person in each squad will lead his or her squad up to the central location in the playing area (mark by a rope or an object). All squads may move at once. The squad leader will draw a card, read the key to see which station the squad must go to, put the card in the other milk crate, and lead the squad to that station. When the squad gets there, they must read the map to find out the state capital and then perform whatever exercise is indicated on the map right there. When that exercise is finished, they return to the central location together, and the squad leader draws another card.

This can be repeated either for a set time limit or until all of the cards are used. Leave the cards faceup so that students can choose to go to each area. When the cards are facedown, sometimes squads don't visit some stations at all.

TARGET 4 CONTINENTS

Why Are We Doing This? To learn the location of the seven continents, the equator, and the Northern and Southern Hemispheres

What Stuff Do We Need? Cones/signs with the name of each continent, the equator, the Northern and Southern Hemispheres, and the names of the oceans; a ball for each student

How Do We Play? The children will discuss the names of the seven continents and their location on Earth. Practice saying the continents and review the use of various movements moving around the continents, with emphasis on north, south, equator, etc.

Once students have an understanding of the names and location of the continents, line students up at the end of the room, side by side. Give each student a colored ball to hold. The children will practice rolling the ball on command and try to hit the continent cones. The teacher will hold up a specific color ball (use four to five different colored balls) and only those children with a specified color will roll at that time. After rolling the ball, the student then travels, using the movement skill designated by the teacher, to that continent.

Children will try to roll their ball from continent to continent for a trip around the world. Encourage children to aim for all seven continents aiming for the closest continent to them, repeating the continent name when they hit that continent.

Children continue to roll the ball and to move from continent to continent. Continent names and pictures are on the cones.

GEOGRAPHY PINBALL

Why Are We Doing This? To review the states, capitals, and their characteristics

What Stuff Do We Need? One foam ball and "fun noodles," or the like, cut into 2-foot sections. (Fun noodles are long 4-inch round Styrofoam floats kids use in the pool in the summertime.) At least four colors of noodles are needed. U.S. map painted on the ground.

How Do We Play? Divide class into four even groups. Each group stands on one side of a U.S. map, which is painted on the court. If you have no map, use any other lines to form a square or rectangle.

This activity starts with one player from each team in the center. The four players "face off" by touching the ball with the noodle, and on the signal "Play!" attempt to strike the ball with the noodle across any team's line except his or her own. Players on the sidelines are also holding noodles and strike the ball back to their team's center player. If the ball crosses a team's line, a point is scored against that team. The point is erased if the team can verbally direct its center player to stand on the state called by the teacher.

Each group of players gets two to three minutes of running time to be center players. Fifteen to 20 seconds are allowed to find the states. Sideline players need to be reminded to stay in their positions (don't block teammates) and to keep one foot OFF the map.

At the end of the allotted time, the points that are accumulated by each team are kept if the team can verbally direct different players on their team to stand on the state called by the teacher (if they made five points, then five different players must stand on the five states the teacher calls out). No matter how many or how few points a team has at the end of time, the score, when students ask, is always awesome!

AMENDMENTS

Why Are We Doing This? To learn/review social studies topics

What Stuff Do We Need? Cones/objects to mark off the activity area

How Do We Play? This activity includes materials that are appropriate for students at these suggested grade levels. However, materials and their relationship to the activity need to be discussed and reviewed with the class in advance. Discuss the Nineteenth Amendment and how it gave women the power to vote. Emphasize the struggle women had in gaining the right to vote. Pose some of the following questions to make sure students understand:

- How do we make important decisions in our country, such as who will be president?
- Before 1920, who got to vote?
- Who didn't have a chance to decide important issues?
- How do we determine if we are for or against an issue that is being voted on in an election?

Form two teams by having two thirds of the class stand on one side of the playing area (these students will be the ones in favor of the amendment) and have the other one third on the other end of the playing area (they are not in favor of the amendment). On the teacher's signal, the team that is in favor of the vote (the majority or larger team) will try to move (teachers determine the movement of travel) to the other end of the playing area without being tagged by the other team. Their goal is to get to the other end of the other team's playing area. This symbolizes the group that successfully got to vote.

When tagged, pro-voters freeze. Have the teams change positions.

PERSONAL CHALLENGE

Why Are We Doing This? To improve directional awareness by locating sites and symbols on a map

What Stuff Do We Need? Map of school grounds being used and/or orienteering booklets (one for every two to three students), answer sheets, controls for each site, and one pen hanging from each control

How Do We Play? Students are placed into groups of two to three. They are given either a map quest (with a white answer sheet), blue booklet (blue answer sheet), or green booklet (green answer sheet). Each map/booklet has a different course of travel. When orienteering, students are working to travel from each location to the next as quickly as possible using a different movement skill each time.

The map should be of the school grounds being used for the course (with landmarks, symbols, etc.). The students are to use the map to find the sites marked with an X. They will use landmarks and symbols on the map to help them find each location. Each site marked with an X has a number next to it (X1–X6 if you have six sites). Before traveling to X1, the students will flip their map over and will read question 1. When they find the correct location of X1, the answer will be found on a "control" hanging at the site. They use the pen hanging from the control to write their answer down on their answer sheet (Answer: heart rate increases). At each station have a physical activity that relates to the stations question (e.g., run in place for 45 seconds as fast as you can and see what happens to your heart rate). They read the question for X2 and travel to that site, and so on.

The blue and green booklets are similar to one another but have different sites to locate and questions to answer (six in each booklet). Each page of the booklet has a picture of a site on your school grounds (i.e., table, soccer goal, bench, tree, etc.). Under that picture will be a numbered question related to any subject and a related physical activity (e.g., What is the state tree of New York? Do 20 jumping jacks and be as wide as possible like a tree). When they find the correct site, a "control" will be there with the answer on it (sugar maple) and a pen hanging to write it down on their answer sheet.

After students have finished locating all sites and answering all questions, they should return to the teacher and, if time permits, try a new orienteering map or booklet.

Controls: Each control should have a pen hanging from it (so students don't have to carry it with them). Write the answers on white paper with a red background for visibility. Write an exercise/task on the control for the students to perform when they arrive at each location (i.e., skipping, jumping jacks, kicking a ball into the soccer goal, etc.). The same locations may be used on the map and in the booklets if you choose, but the students must know the correct answer to write down on their answer sheet when looking at the control. Write the blue booklet answers in blue, green booklet answers in green, and map quest answers in black. Make sure to place the correct question number next to each answer.

PLAYGROUND AEROBICS

Why Are We Doing This? To create a map and key and to reinforce map skills

What Stuff Do We Need? The teacher should draw the playground on a sheet of paper. This should include a map key. The students also need a map, pencil, and crayons.

How Do We Play? The teacher posts the map on the chalkboard. This map is exactly like the map she or he hands out to the class.

- The first thing the teacher asks the students to do is to number the 10 places they would like to play on the playground.
- Second, have the students look at the map key and use the symbols for climbing, sliding, hanging, and swinging to show what they would like to do at each number they have placed on the map.
- Then, have the students use the locomotor skills listed in the map key to show how they would like to get from place to place.
- Finally, have all the students work together with you and color code the map key symbols. (Make sure to use different colors for each symbol.) Once the symbols are colored coded, apply the appropriate color to the symbols they have put on their map.

Take the maps outside and break the class into groups of four or five and have them try each other's maps.

RACE 4 THE PRESIDENCY

Why Are We Doing This? To learn about the electoral college and electoral race

What Stuff Do We Need? A "cutout" of each state with the number of electoral votes on the back, three presidential name tags, a large playing area with clearly marked boundaries on each end

How Do We Play? Ask for three volunteers to be the presidential candidates that stand in the middle of the playing area. The rest of the class is each assigned a state and instructed to line up at one end of the playing area. Each state name tag has a number under the state name that represents the number of electoral votes that state receives in an election.

When the presidential candidates yell "the race is on," the states will try to move in different ways past the candidates to the other end of the playing area without getting tagged by the candidates. If a state (student) gets tagged, it belongs to the candidate who tagged it. The state must then help its candidate capture more states until all are captured.

Each candidate and his or her group of states will then add up their electoral votes to determine who will be the next U.S. president.

Sample Questions:

- Does it really matter which state each candidate wins in the electoral race?
- How many votes are necessary to win the electoral college?
- Who won the election?

This is an outstanding activity to educate youngsters about the importance of voting.

CAPTAIN CAPITAL

Why Are We Doing This? To review the states and their capitals

What Stuff Do We Need? A small ball (foam or tennis ball) for each pair, paddles to strike with if you choose to, large-scale maps (preferably laminated and made by the students in advance) of the United States to be placed around the playing area walls

How Do We Play? Prior to students arriving, hang the enlarged maps around the playing area that the students created in advance. Randomly assign a pair of students a map to work with. Give each pair of students one small ball to use for striking.

- On the teacher's signal, each student will use their hand or a paddle to strike the ball in different ways toward the wall (use the right and the left hand if not using the paddle).
- When the ball hits a state, the students are asked to recite the capital of that state. Students are not to hit the ball continuously. They should catch the ball after they hit it. If they do not know the capital or the state, their partner can help them.
- Each student is to alternate with his or her partner.
- The teacher can specify to hit the ball to a high level; or to a low level; to the right, or to the left; with the right hand, left hand, backward, under a body part; in the center of the state; or anywhere allowing for different patterns of striking.

This activity is a whole lot of fun for kids to learn the states and capitals.

CHASING STATES

Why Are We Doing This? To learn about state capitals

What Stuff Do We Need? Cones/objects to mark off a safe playing area

How Do We Play? Children are in scattered formation within the playing area. Identify two thirds as chasers or "its." On the teachers "go," signal the chasers to pursue the other students trying to tag them softly (start off with slower movements and progress to more active; i.e., slide, grapevine, skip, etc.). When someone is tagged, he or she must freeze immediately.

To unfreeze the frozen, free runners must stand in front of the frozen players. The frozen student says the name of a state, and the unfrozen student must say the name of the capital of that state. If the answer is wrong, then they can keep trying, try another state name, or they could slide over to another student who is frozen and get help from them. During the guessing process, these students cannot be tagged.

DIRECTION TOSS

Why Are We Doing This? To learn cardinal directions of north, south, east and west in making a compass rose with the equipment

What Stuff Do We Need? Beanbags, hacky sack, balls, dots, mouse pads (modify equipment with what you have)

How Do We Play? Children are instructed to pick up a ball, hacky sack, dot, and a beanbag and to put the equipment in the following order: the dot is in the center, the ball is to the east, the hacky sack is to the north, the beanbag is to the west, and the student is to the south. The teacher will review the directions located on each wall of the playing area. The teacher will call out cardinal directions, and the children will practice tossing equipment up and catching it. The teacher directions will not include saying the equipment, but will use a direction: that is, east will mean tossing the ball, north will indicate tossing the hacky sack, west will indicate tossing the beanbag, etc. Children can be given two cardinal directions to use at the same time.

Next have the children practice tossing to a target, giving directions such as "Using the west equipment (beanbag), toss to land in the north equipment (hacky sack)." Have children increase their distance when successful. Children will be given a mouse pad to be placed in the northeast corner that will also be used as a target. Children will use the east (ball) and west (beanbag) equipment to hit the targets. Encourage children to throw equipment to a target that is similar in shape, that is, throwing the ball to the ring and the beanbag to the mouse pad.

STATE LOCATION

Why Are We Doing This? To reinforce the locations of the states

What Stuff Do We Need? Strips of paper with the names of the states printed on them and an overhead with an outline of the United States for students to check with as needed during the activity

How Do We Play? Have the students start at the edge of the playing area. Each one draws a slip of paper with the name of a state. When the teacher says, "Go," the students jump, skip, or crawl to the area where their state should be. To figure out who they should stand by, the students ask the other students which states they represent until every state is in the correct spot.

BUDDY STATES

Why Are We Doing This? To locate the 50 states on the U.S. map

What Stuff Do We Need? Large map of the United States painted on the outside blacktop or other area, index cards with a state identified on each one, tube socks or other fabric long enough to tie ankles together, small map of United States with states identified

How Do We Play? Students are paired up with a partner, scattered around the general space, and will use the tube sock to tie their ankles together. The teacher should encourage each group to discuss a strategy they will use to help them move together across the map.

Give the students an opportunity to practice a variety of movements (i.e., back to back, side to side, etc.) by moving all around the general space. Once the students have practiced moving together, start the game.

The teacher will toss all the cards with the states on them up in the air so that they land scattered all over the area. On a signal, the partners (with ankles tied) begin by picking up one card, going to the map, and placing it on the correct location, and then continuing by retrieving another card, and taking it to be placed on the map.

The game continues until all the cards have been correctly placed on the large map. It is best to tape "cheat sheets" at both sides of the map so that students can use them as a reference if they are unsuccessful in locating the state on the large map. The game can be repeated numerous times using different movements or different partner movements.

CRUISIN' CONTINENTS

Why Are We Doing This? To learn/review information regarding the seven continents on our planet

What Stuff Do We Need? Up-tempo music, poly spots/paper plates or hula hoops (one for each student), a world map, color-coded continent cutouts made of seven different colors of paper, 12 copies of each continent

How Do We Play? Place the continents along the basketball boundaries of the playing area. Inside the area place more than enough poly spots/plates for each one of the students.

The students are given directions to stay inside of the court, moving safely away from the slippery pieces of paper on the outside line. Also instruct them to move without bumping or pushing each other. Review the continents on the world map. Instruct the students to move the way the teacher directs when the music is playing. When the music stops, students find a poly spot/plate. The teacher asks a question or states a fact about one of the seven continents (e.g., On which continent do we live?). After the question, students will walk on the boundary line to find the continent and point to it. They have a time limit, and no more than two people can point to the same continent at one time. The teacher counts down from 15, and students must be pointing at the continent at the end of this time.

Ask the students to identify the color continent to which they are pointing. Assess their responses. If there are incorrect responses, discuss the correct answer and continue with another movement to music.

Sample questions:

- What continent is the farthest south and has really cold temperatures?
- What continent is home to the Koala bear? The kangaroo? The platypus?
- What continent has the largest land area?
- What continent is home to the countries of Spain, France, and Italy?

Alter the questions in conjunction with what is taught at each grade level.

STATE LINE

Why Are We Doing This? To encourage the child to practice balancing activities while learning the states in the United States

What Stuff Do We Need? One long jump rope per child, a map of the United States, laminated individual states in the United States

How Do We Play? Have each student get a long jump rope and select a state to form in their self space. Instruct each child to make the state's shape with their long jump rope. Try using different balancing skills to move along the state line without falling off.

Additional skills to do at their rope:

- Walking forward, backward, sideways
- Moving at high, medium, and low levels
- Moving with two, three, or four different body parts touching the floor
- Traveling and balancing an object (e.g., beanbag) on their head, back of hand, or shoulder as they move

After working at their own individual state, have students travel around to other states. Have the students skip (or use various locomotor skills) to each state, name the state and the state capital. (Let half of the class do this, while the other half stays at their state to see if the state and capital are named correctly, then switch.)

ACTION-PACKED HEALTH

VEGGIE PIGOUT

Why Are We Doing This? To encourage children to eat healthy foods

What Stuff Do We Need? Index with different foods on each card (healthy and nonhealthy foods), one jump rope for each student

How Do We Play? Scatter the cards around the playing area throughout the general space. Turn them upside down so the foods can't be seen. Have each child begin at any card with a jump rope in hand.

- Students turn a card over and if they think it is a "healthy" food, then they pick it up and move upright to another card.
- If it is an "unhealthy" food, then the students need to be "frozen" while squatting until another student tags them.
- Before they can be freed, they must name a "healthy" food in the same food group as the food they picked up that was unhealthy and they must move to another food by jumping rope to make themselves healthy and to get to their new food.
- While the students are moving, the teacher will call out a specific pathway (straight, curved, zigzag), level (low, medium, high), or direction (forward, backward, sideways) for the students to move in every few minutes.

Excellent activity for a "supersized society" to recognize appropriate foods for health.

ACTION 911

Why Are We Doing This? To gain an understanding of the roles and responsibilities of those individuals who serve our community and respond to 911 emergency calls

What Stuff Do We Need? Four to six carpet squares (or adaptation), two flat mats, marked area or restraining line

How Do We Play? Form two equal teams and have them sit behind a restraining line.

- Have them imagine they are in a burning house.
- Each team has two or three rescuers who each have a carpet square.
- The rescuers are standing on the fire safe spot, the gym mats on the opposite side of the activity area.
- On the command, Rescue 911, the rescuers run to the burning house and rescue each person one by one. The rescuer must pull the victim to safety.
- "Victims" must remain sitting or kneeling on the carpet square throughout the entire rescue. This continues until everyone on the team is rescued. If need be rescuers may work together to pull the victim to safety.
- This continues until everyone is rescued.

No one ever worries about which team wins. The true fun is getting your turn to rescue. By the time everyone has had a turn to rescue everyone has had a blast.

ESCAPE ROUTE

Why Are We Doing This? To learn importance of escape routes in houses or apartments

What Stuff Do We Need? Jump ropes, mats, blindfolds, cones, and other things that students can use to build an obstacle course (modify accordingly)

How Do We Play? Have the equipment (listed above) set out into four safe areas of the playing area. Divide students into three to four groups. When they get to the area, they are to work together to design an obstacle course that utilizes all of the equipment in their area.

Explain to the students that in order to safely get out of your house during a fire, you may have to negotiate different obstacles during that escape. Have the students practice going through course.

Variations:

- Have the students go through blindfolded.
- Have the students pair up. One student is blindfolded, the other is not. The student that has use of his or her sight must give directions to the blinded student about how to get through the obstacle course. Time the students.
- Designate two thirds of the obstacles as doors. Make sure they check the door for heat before proceeding.

FOOD GROUP JAM

Why Are We Doing This? To reinforce nutrition concepts

What Stuff Do We Need? Six numbered cones (1–6), 360 food cards on plain white index cards (60 per food group), six game boards: each game board uses two pieces of #10 tag board and 36 index cards of various colors with physical fitness activities written on them, and each half of the board should be laminated and taped together on the back side

How Do We Play? Separate the class into six or more even teams. Each team lines up behind one of the numbered cones. (The game board is in front of the cone and the food cards are spread out in the center circle of the playing area.) Player #1 in each group does the designated movement skill—hop, skip, gallop, slide, etc.—to the center circle and selects a food card. He or she then brings the card back and places it under the correct food group, over one of the physical fitness cards. Player #1 then leads his or her group (except for player #2) in the fitness activity that was covered up with the food card. He or she then brings the food card back to the game board and places it under the correct food group. Player #2 then leads the group in the activity that he or she covered up, while player #3 heads to the center circle. The group continues getting food cards and leading activities until the game board is completely filled.

NUTRITION DRIBBLE

Why Are We Doing This? To practice reading food labels and the correct number of grams of fats/proteins/carbohydrates in a single serving

What Stuff Do We Need? Enough nutrition labels from various foods for each student in the class. Food labels should show different numbers of carbohydrate, protein, and fat grams. Master list of all nutrition labels and the number of fat, protein, and carbohydrate grams per serving. Balls of various sizes so each student may choose. Cones/objects to place nutrition labels under.

How Do We Play? The students will review the general form of a nutrition label off of any food. A short discussion of the importance of carbohydrates and proteins plus a small amount of fat in the diet needs to be reviewed.

- Each student will choose the size ball that he or she is comfortable with and the teacher will assign each child a number of grams of carbohydrates or fat from the master list of food labels.
- On the "go" signal, the music begins and all students must dribble to the different cones and look under them until they find the nutrition label that has their designated number of carbohydrate, protein, or fat grams.

- Upon finding the right label they dribble to the teacher; show him or her the label; and state the food, the designated number of carbohydrate, protein, or fat grams, and whether it is a healthy food or not according to carbohydrate, protein, and fat content.
- After completion of the task, they dribble the label back to the cone and return to the teacher for a new food!

What a great activity to reiterate the importance of nutrition labeling reading!

RECYCLING ROCK-A-THON

Why Are We Doing This? To learn about recycling

What Stuff Do We Need? Three trash cans or buckets; clean trash such as paper, plastic, and aluminum; three color-coded signs—one marked paper, one marked plastic, and one marked aluminum

How Do We Play? Have students spread out in the general space. Place the three labeled trash cans (labeled paper, plastic, and aluminum) at different locations around the playing area. Make each sign a different color for students who cannot read.

Mix up the trash and spread it out all around the playing area and the three cans. Remind students what it means to recycle and why it is important. Show examples of each type of trash that can be recycled and explain the recycling containers to them. When the teacher says go, the students are to pick up any piece of trash and place it in the correct labeled trash can by traveling using the movement skill that the teacher calls out. The teacher can vary the movement skills by using different directions (forward, backward), different levels (high, medium, and low), different speeds, and different pathways for the students to travel.

"HOPPY" FEELINGS

Why Are We Doing This? To allow the students to express their emotions with "life"

What Stuff Do We Need? Six "feelings plates" for each student in the class (six blank paper plates for each student to put one feeling on each plate and decorate with faces expressing that emotion)

How Do We Play? Have students find their own space. Remind them that they must remain in their own personal space throughout the activity.

- Have students place their "feeling plates" in a scattered formation around them.
- Review the skill of hopping.
- Call out an event, such as "I am having a birthday party!"
- Have the students hop in different ways on the face that shows the feelings they would have if they were having a birthday party.
- Continue giving different situations and have the students hop to whichever face symbolizes how they would feel in that situation. Different types of hops can include hopping on the right/left foot; hopping at a high, medium, or low level; hopping hard/soft, fast/slow; etc.
- Use other movement concepts to express emotion. For example, sad would be hopping slowly at a low level, happy might be hopping quickly and lightly, mad might be hopping in a zigzag pathway with strong force while still traveling toward one of the smiley faces.

End the activity by discussing the importance of expressing their feelings.

HEART-HEALTHY FOOD CHALLENGE

Why Are We Doing This? To identify which foods are considered healthy for the body/heart, and which ones are not

What Stuff Do We Need? Small containers/garbage pails (three per group), posters (three for each container), sign to designate which color each group is, small cones/objects (one for each group and to mark a center circle), under/over sticks (as many as the center circle needs), index cards with pictures of food as well as food name (as many as you can think of)

How Do We Play? Students should be split up into groups of three to four that each sit behind a small cone around the edge of the playing area. On that cone should be the color of the team. In the center of the playing area, create a circle marked with cones and hurdles. Inside the circle, place all of the food cards with pictures facedown on the floor. Each card should be made with a team color on it so that there are equal cards for each team. For example, if a card has a picture of a candy bar on it, there should be a blue one, red one, etc.

At each color home base, place the three containers with their respective signs on them. The signs should say "Healthy food," "Food to eat only sometimes," and "Not sure." You can also put a smiley face, a frowning face, and a face with a straight line for those who have trouble reading.

On the signal, the first partner will run toward the center circle and crawl underneath the hurdle to enter the circle. There, the child will pick up a card of his or her team's color. The student will determine whether it is a healthy or a "only sometimes" food. Once the child figures this out, he or she needs to jump over the hurdle (to get out of the circle) and run to one of the three labeled containers. There the child drops the card into the container that he or she feels is the correct one. Then the student will run back to his or her group and give the next student a "high five," then the second partner continues to do the same. Make sure that there are LOTS of different cards inside the circle.

Once all of the team's cards are gone, the team should re-check each container to see if they have the correct color cards and to make any last minute changes. Then the teacher can discuss which foods should be in each container.

MOTOR SAFETY

Why Are We Doing This? To learn safety rules and knowledge of the road by going through a driving course using scooters/bicycles/tricycles, etc. This activity is designed to introduce driving and safety to students in a "pretend" setting. Students learn why it is important to obey all traffic laws and understand the consequences of disobeying traffic laws.

What Stuff Do We Need? Scooters, bicycles, tricycles, cones, signs, gutters, ropes, jump ropes, make-believe tunnel, floor mats (whatever works!)

How Do We Play? The driving range can be set up in a variety of different ways. The teacher needs to ensure that there is enough allotted space for all the children to be active without waiting in line for a turn. This activity would be best used with small groups or large outdoor areas where several activity areas can be set up and supervised.

- The teacher explains what is appropriate and inappropriate for the driving range. For example, no standing on scooters/bicycles/tricycles, no tailgating, safely park scooters/bicycles/tricycles while parking in lot, etc. While students watch and listen, the teacher must walk through the course explaining what he or she expects of the students.
- The teacher walks the students through the driving range and explains each feature. Stop signs, one way signs, and speed limit signs are posted around the course.
- Students must obey the signs or they will be given a traffic ticket. The course includes a freeway, a car wash, a tunnel, and a couple of different parking lots.
- Students must park their scooters/bicycles/tricycles in designated parking lots and perform particular skills for that day. These skills can include various rolls on a mat, a rope swing and land on both feet, and/or a balance beam walk down a rope.
- When students complete the driving range, they can begin again.

- The students' goal is to earn their own drivers license, so they must be very careful and safe to do a good job.
- Traffic tickets will be issued to students who do not follow the rules of the road. If any student gets two or more tickets, he or she will not earn a drivers license or safety license (teacher's choice).

Whew . . . we've all seen drivers on the road that could use a dose of this activity!

HOUSE OF PANCAKES

Why Are We Doing This? To improve creativity and health education

What Stuff Do We Need? Poly spots/paper plates (any color, any size) one per partner group, *If You Give a Pig a Pancake* by Laura Numeroff, examples of food grains

How Do We Play? Discuss the elements of the basic food pyramid and different foods (particularly grains) that you put into your body. Show the book *If You Give a Pig a Pancake* by Laura Numeroff, and read the story to the class. Allow the students time to guess what is going to happen when the pig is given a pancake in the story. Discuss the different food groups on the food pyramid and into which group the pancake would fall.

- Have the students find a partner and use a single poly spot to represent the pancake.
- Allow each student time to explore and devise a variety of ways to get the pancake to his or her partner.
- Examples include rolling the pancake, let the pancake land in a hoop made by their partner's arms, dropkick the pancake, overhand throw, underhand throw, let the pancake land on a body part, Frisbee throw, etc.
- At the conclusion, allow the students to create a different ending for the story that would involve the activities they used with their partners.
- Allow the students to choose a different food and discuss its place in the food pyramid and an activity to go along with the food.

Students can write their conclusions to the story for a writing assignment when they return to the classroom.

LOW-FAT, HIGH-FAT

Why Are We Doing This? To learn about fat in the diet

What Stuff Do We Need? Pictures of food dishes mounted on heavy poster board (about 5-inch by 5-inch in size), cones/objects for general space

How Do We Play? Place pictures of different food dishes around the playing area.

- The students begin to move around general space using any movement pattern.
- When the children hear the signal they are to pick up a picture closest to them.
- After looking at it they need to determine whether it is a high- or low-fat food.
- After making that decision they are to move through the room in a predetermined movement pattern (i.e., high fat means to slide sideways, low fat means to skip forward). They hold their picture above their heads while moving so you can see them.
- On your signal they put the picture down, continue to move freely through the general space, and pick up a new picture on your signal.

This is a great way for you to check for nutritional understanding of your students.

PASSWORD PROTECTION

Why Are We Doing This? To teach kids about child abduction

What Stuff Do We Need? Five pieces of paper with passwords written on them

How Do We Play? This activity is very similar to Amoeba Tag. Five (or a number of your choice) students are given a private password (they are the "adults"). Each of the other children is given one of the five passwords. They aren't allowed to tell anyone their password.

As the children move through general space using different movement patterns, the adults go around the room, approaching each child, and saying their password. If an adult finds a child with the same password, that child must "attach" to the adult, and continue moving around the room in search of more students with the same password.

This continues until all have found the adult with the matching password.

STOP, DROP, AND ROLL

Why Are We Doing This? To teach emergency procedures

What Stuff Do We Need? Nothing

How Do We Play?

Activity 1: Moving in General Space

- Students are spread out in general space in a safe manner (arms distance apart).
- On teacher's command, students walk in general space until they hear the signal "stop." The students immediately stop.
- The students continue to walk in general space again. This time the teacher calls out "drop and roll."
- The students then practice falling safely to the floor and then roll like a log three or four times on the floor until the teacher gives the signal to continue with a traveling movement (i.e., skipping, galloping, etc.).
- The teacher can ask the children to call out the words "stop," "drop," and "roll," immediately after the teacher says each word.

Activity 2: Tag Game

- Three or four students are chosen as taggers. Give those students a red sock stuffed with tissue paper.
- When the taggers tag the runners with the socks and say "fire," the tagged runner must shout "stop, drop, and roll," and then perform the movements (stop, drop, and roll) before continuing to play the game.
- After a few minutes, new taggers are selected and the game continues.

MAKE IT HAPPEN

To ensure success, it is advantageous for you, the teacher, to follow up and make sure that the movement reminders at the beginning of this chapter are in place. The "Movement Reminders Checklist for Academic Action" (see Resources) will help in this regard.

LET'S WRAP IT UP

It's no wonder Mr. Miller, our second-year teacher at Oakville Elementary School, is so successful! With the abundance of incredibly awesome movement-integrated academic activities in this chapter, you too can keep your kids "loving learning." From a "Creature Feature" science activity to a language arts "Sentence Detectives" game, your students will be grinning from ear to ear and moving from head to toe.

Remember, every student in your classroom is a unique and different individual from anyone else in your room. Each child learns differently. You will be amazed at the success you will have when subject matter is taught through a multitude of modalities. Even that hard-to-reach learner responds! And learns!

So, go out there, touch those students' lives, and have fun.

5

Subject Matter Template Games

The least expensive education is to profit from the mistakes of ourselves and others.

—Anonymous

LET'S BEGIN

How many times have you taught a lesson and it took forever to get the directions straight to the kids so they understood what to do? Frequently, teachers get frustrated as this process can take up a whole period or even longer. When much of precious instructional time is used up in the setup, many teachers will not do an activity as there's just too much content to cover and not enough time! Subject matter template games to the rescue! Why not teach your students how to play the game and weave the content through the same setup? Once the kids know how to play the game, teach them another content standard through the same activity. This is a great way to use your instructional time much more wisely; plus, the children are learning by doing multiple content standards and having healthy fun, too.

CHECK THIS OUT

Have you noticed that if we, as teachers, were to cover everything that is mandated by educational laws, we would never leave our schools? We would be teaching 24/7!

Mr. Nichols, a Cardiff Elementary School special education teacher in Fairfield, Florida, has figured out that if he focuses on game templates in activities, he won't have to reteach the "how" to play. Once the children learn the format, much of the instructional time is cut way down.

One will often see him out on the playground with the kids up to some new adventure. For example, once he has taught "cup searches," the children play this activity on a regular basis and just "switch it up" to the desired content.

The kids are happy, Mr. Nichols is happy, and the academic scores reflect this. His students remember so much more as they are doing the learning.

WHY EVEN BOTHER?

Asking "Why bother?" is basically the same as saying "Don't give us more instructional time." Duh. What teacher would ever say that? One of the biggest complaints of teachers is there just isn't enough time. Utilize your time to the max!

The following are the six Fit4Learning A.C.T.I.V.E. Standards. Along with your state standards or national standards, the Fit4Learning A.C.T.I.V.E. Standards are based on neuroscience. If you want your students to remember the content in the little time you have with them, use the Fit4Learning A.C.T.I.V.E. Standards to your benefit.

(A)erobic Integration: Knows the importance of aerobic activity to academic achievement and physical health. Neurotransmitters primed for learning are released and available because of this Fit4Learning integration in curriculum.

(C)ooperative and Character Components: Understands the value of working together and the meaning of character skills. The combinations of these components are practiced throughout the Fit4Learning environment.

(T)hinking Without Chairs: Knows that intrinsic learning occurs when the student is engaged in the process. Multiple modalities are utilized when there is a shift in the delivery of instruction from sedentary to Fit4Learning active.

(I)nvolvement by All: Comprehends that to learn, one must be involved. The Fit4Learning classrooms are high-participation venues.

(V)oluntary Exercise: Knows that to acquire the full benefits to the brain, one must "want" to do the exercise. Fit4Learning instructional lessons are creatively planned, making fitness fun so kids love to move.

(E)ating Healthy: Understands that healthy food is vital to learning and can distinguish the "good stuff" from the junk. Fit4Learning kids demonstrate a desire to eat healthy.

Benefits of the Fit4Learning A.C.T.I.V.E. Standards:

- Students' brains are primed for learning
- Children's bodies are fit to learn actively
- Addresses core standards and physical education standards simultaneously
- Utilizes maximum movement with minimal equipment
- Fights obesity via active lessons
- Learning is achieved through multiple modalities
- Students acquire the skills to get along
- Involvement is by all; no child is left out
- Fit4Learning schools are leaders of the wellness laws and policies
- Happy kids, happy teachers, happy schools result

MAKE IT HAPPEN

It's now time to play Subject Matter Template Games. Whatever the grade-level standards you are teaching, just tweak the lesson to fit your needs. It's as easy as A, B, C.

FIT4LEARNING FLOOR TAPE GAMES

Why Are We Doing This? To reinforce multiple content standards Grades K–5

What Stuff Do We Need? Red floor tape, word tiles, fraction tiles, decimal blocks, beanbags, yarn balls, playing cards; add anything depending on grade level and diversity of game

How Do We Play? Arrange four tape squares approximately with 2 feet per side. Place the squares equal distance on floor from each other.

- Place various objects in each tape square
- Divide class into four groups, one behind each tape square
- A player can take only one object at a time
- All players are in movement depending on locomotor skill the teacher has decided

- When the teacher gives the cue to stop, he or she will have each team solve the various content standard problems
- Play short games
- For larger classes or variety, add more tape squares
- Players cannot guard their home square or throw objects

Math:

Place multiple fraction tiles and decimal blocks in each square. Students are to take away a fraction tile from home square and come back with a decimal block. When music stops or on stop cue, students match the appropriate fraction with the appropriate decimal. In addition, playing cards can be placed in squares facedown. Students are to sit in a sit-up position with toes on tape. On teacher's cue, students sit up, turn a card over, and add up all teammates cards. Whoever adds them up gets the pile. Repeat numerous times.

Science:

Place various beanbags in square. Each color beanbag can represent a different part of the water cycle. Repeat same procedures.

Tape Games

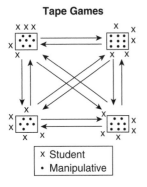

x Student
• Manipulative

Language Arts:

Place appropriate word tiles in square. On stop cue, have children create complete sentences with tiles. In addition, students can alphabetize words. Have students recite their sentences to other groups. Repeat same procedures.

Social Studies:

Place various colored yarn balls in square. Each color represents a different aspect of government such as Democrats, Republicans, and Independents. Repeat same procedures.

Health:

Place various items in squares that represent healthy foods and those that represent unhealthy. For example, yogurt containers, potato chip bags, skim milk containers, coke cans, etc. Repeat same procedures.

FIT4LEARNING CUP SEARCH GAMES

Why Are We Doing This? To reinforce multiple content standard Grades K–5

What Stuff Do We Need? Red floor tape, word tiles, multiples blocks; add anything desirable depending on grade level and diversity of game

How Do We Play? Teacher makes five tape squares equal distance apart from each other; approximately 20 yards apart. Students are put into five groups. Teacher tosses bunches of cups all over the gym or playing area floor.

- Challenge students to place cups open side up 1 meter apart, timing them
- Next, toss up objects such as word tiles
- Challenge students to put cup over only one tile; covering all the tiles
- Students leave their home one or two kids at a time
- Students can turn over one cup at a time and on each trip
- Each grade level there is a different criterion
- Teams that end up with the most criteria met win

Cup Search Games

x Students
△ Cup

Math:

Place multiple color number blocks under each cup. Each team represents a multiple of 3, 4, 5, 7, or 11. When the teacher cues to stop, all students count up their blocks. Repeat.

Science:

Place various colored blocks and tiles under cups. Certain colors of blocks will represent precipitation, condensation, evaporation, and freezing. Play game with same procedures.

Language Arts:

Place various word tiles that are "parts of speech" under the scattered cups. Play game with same procedures. On the teacher's cue to stop, children count up how many "parts of speech" they have in their home square.

Social Studies:

Place various objects under the cups in scattered formation. Students are reminded about fairness, individual rights, diversity, and the common good of working together.

Health:

Place various cards under cups that represent different parts of the food groups. Groups can be fruits, vegetables, dairy products, meats, oils, and grains.

FIT4LEARNING CLOTHESPIN AND CLOTHESLINE GAMES

Why Are We Doing This? To reinforce multiple content standards Grades K–5

What Stuff Do We Need? Clothespins, clothesline, word tiles, and laminated flash cards; add anything desirable depending on grade level and diversity of game   *need clothespins*

How Do We Play? Teacher lays out one of the ropes across the gym or playing-area floor. Students are instructed to stay away from the rope. For example, they can leap across the rope, but cannot land on or stand over it. Explain to the students the safety hazard if they jump on the rope.

- Teacher tosses flash cards all over the playing area.
- Students are indicated to spread out the flash cards facedown 1 meter apart.
- Students find a partner "side by side."
- Teacher picks two students who will be the "enders." The enders are instructed to pull the rope up in the air on the teacher's cue or when the music stops.
- Object of the game: to create number lines, integer lines, and timelines on the rope.
- When music stops or on the teacher's cue after students are moving to a locomotor skill, one of the two of each partnered group picks up a flash card and places it on rope. The teacher has announced "enders" so the rope is waist high. The student that picked up the card stands behind the rope; the partner is in front checking for accuracy.
- Switch partner. Repeat.

Clothespins and Clothesline Game

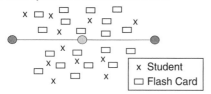

x Student
□ Flash Card

Math:

Scatter flash cards according to directions. Integrate integer, fraction, decimal, rounding, and any other math content you desire! Be sure and clothespin the "zero" in the center of the rope.

jump bands will fit true over the ends of the zone

Science:

Here's a great idea! Use two ropes utilizing four enders. The ropes cross perpendicular at the center. Science flash cards are scattered all over play area. Follow directions of game; students pick up a flash card and clothespin to the correct classification: mammals, birds, insects, or fish.

Language Arts:

Try using the word tiles and create sentences or match up the parts of speech.

Social Studies:

Scatter the presidents' flash cards and create a historical timeline.

Health:

Have students place pictures of "healthy" foods and "nonhealthy" foods on face of flash cards. Scatter randomly all over floor facedown about 1 meter apart. Have students move around cards. On the teacher's cue, students pick up a card and clothespin at appropriate place on rope.

FIT4LEARNING ALL-RUN PROBLEM-SOLVING GAMES

Why Are We Doing This? To reinforce multiple content standards Grades K–5

What Stuff Do We Need? Four bases, soccer ball, word tiles, beanbags, 10 poly spots, fraction and decimal blocks; add anything desirable depending on grade level and diversity of game

How Do We Play?

- Set up a softball-type diamond and distribute 10 poly spots in the outfield.
- Divide the class into kicking and fielding teams.
- A good number for each team is 10 players.
- Kicking team lines up behind the backstop or in a safe area.
- The first batter kicks either a rolled (pitched) or stationary ball into fair territory and runs around the bases without stopping.
- All members of the kicking team follow in single file (no passing allowed).
- Change sides after four or five kickers.
- Direct students to play different positions each inning.
- Once students understand game rules, divide class into four teams on two fields (for larger classes, make more teams). Smaller teams allow the game to be played with all students having a turn "at bat" before the other team is up.
- The fielding team gets the kicking team "out" by solving the content standard problem by runners tossing objects (explanation below) and by throwing the kicked ball to a different player in each of the 10 poly spots.
- Each player reaching home plate before an "out" is declared scores one run for the team.

Math:

All-Run Problem-Solving Games

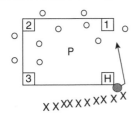

The running team throws a beanbag to outfield. The members of the outfield team are each standing on a poly spot at least 10 feet apart from each other. Each color beanbag represents a different amount of money. Once the running team kicks the soccer ball and starts running the bases, the outfield team finds a beanbag and runs it to the pitcher. The members of the outfield team add up the amount of money they have and return to their poly spots. One outfielder starts throwing the soccer ball until it ends up at the pitcher's spot. Then the fielding team yells out how much money they have!

Science:

The game is played the same except the running team doesn't throw anything. The outfield team has to switch and run to a different poly spot. Once the soccer ball is retrieved by the outfield, each outfielder needs to transport the ball to the next player using a different mode, for example, throw, kick, roll, bounce, etc.

Language Arts:

The game is played the same way as the math template game; however, students throw one word tile to the outfield. Outfielders alphabetize words at the pitcher's spot then proceed as indicated.

Social Studies:

The running team represents the settlers in the colonies, while the outfielders are the British. As the running team runs the bases before the soccer ball gets to the pitcher, they are chanting, "The British are coming, the British are coming."

Health:

The game is played the same; however, each beanbag represents a fruit or vegetable. The outfielders will figure out what healthy foods they have in their shopping carts.

FIT4LEARNING WHO'S GOT IT? GAMES

Why Are We Doing This? To reinforce multiple content standards Grades K–5

What Stuff Do We Need? Yarn balls, beanbags, math tiles; add anything desirable depending on grade level and diversity of game

How Do We Play?

- Set up a playing field where there are two end lines, one on each end. The larger the playing field, the better, as it offers the students more running space.
- Half of the class is on one team; the other half is on the other team.
- Object of the game is to get from one side to the other without being tagged.
- Hidden in each runner's hand is an object depending on the content being taught.
- The players who make it to the other side without being tagged meet and figure out "what" made it to safety area. The students who are tagged complete 10 curl-ups or other teacher-specified exercise while totals are accounted for.

Who's Got It? Game

Math:

Each runner has a math tile. Each digit can only be used once unless class size allows for duplicates or triplicates. The students who make it across add up the numbers. Strive for the highest numbers!

Science:

Each student has a yarn ball that represents a different animal. What animals do you have in your zoo?

Language Arts:

Each student has a word tile. Can a complete sentence be made with the runners who make it across?

Social Studies:

Each beanbag represents a different culture. What is the makeup of your group?

Health:

Yellow yarn balls and beanbags are bad fats; green yarn balls and beanbags are good fats. What do you end up with more of?

FIT4LEARNING JUMP ROPE RHYMES AND GAMES

Why Are We Doing This? To reinforce multiple content standards Grades K–5

What Stuff Do We Need? Fit4Learning jump ropes; add anything desirable depending on grade level and diversity of game

jump bands will work in classroom

How Do We Play?
- Preferably five students per group
- Two enders per rope/group
- Alternate enders periodically
- Set up challenges and chants
- Have fun

Math:

> Apples, peaches, pears, and plums
> Tell me when your birthday comes.

A great idea is to jump "hot peppers" (or really fast skipping) and say the months of the year (January, February, March, etc.), trying to not get out until you reach the month of your birthday, and then count each day off until your "birthday" is reached.

Science:

> Dum-dum dodo, catch me if you can.
> I can run faster than _____ can.

The verse is sung, and then the person enters the rope and picks someone else. I would have to say it's the most common jump rope rhyme that is used at recess.

Language Arts:

(Rhyming Words): Three Blind Mice

> A horse, a flea, and three blind mice,
> sat on a curbstone shooting dice.
> The horse, he slipped and fell on the flea.
> The flea said, "Whoops, there's a horse on me."

Social Studies:

> George Washington never told a lie.
> How many cherries were in that pie?
> 1, 2, 3, 4 . . .

(Count until the jumper messes up.)

Health:

The two holding the rope chant

> Peel a banana upside down,
> see if you can touch the ground.

(The jumper tries to touch the ground without being tripped by the rope.)

> If you spell your name correct,
> you will get another chance . . .

The jumper then spells his or her name, including saying "capital" for uppercase letters of his or her name. If the jumper trips or messes up the spelling, it's another jumper's turn.

FIT4LEARNING BALLOON BONANZA GAMES

Why Are We Doing This? To reinforce multiple content standards Grades K–5

What Stuff Do We Need? Balloons, ropes, yarn balls or beanbags; add anything desirable depending on grade level and diversity of game

How Do We Play? Just blow up your balloons and you're good to go.

Math:

Start off with everyone in a circle, facing inward, hands behind back. The objective is for everyone to be in the center, keeping all balloons afloat. Put between zero and three balloons in people's hands behind their backs. Participants should not let on to others how many they have. The leader starts by trying to keep three balloons afloat in the center. When it becomes difficult, the leader calls somebody's name and says, "X, I need your help!" That person comes in with all his or her balloons and helps until it becomes difficult and then calls, "Y, I need your help!" If a balloon falls on the ground, it must be picked up by someone in the center and kept afloat. Count how many balloons are up in air.

Science:

Two to three inflated balloons per person are needed and a stopwatch. Each person has a balloon, with the rest in a nearby pile. Everyone begins bouncing their balloons in the air. Every five seconds, another balloon is added. See how long the group can keep the balloons bouncing before receiving six penalties. A penalty is announced loudly by the leader when a balloon hits the floor, or once on the floor, if is not back in play within five seconds. The leader keeps a cumulative score by shouting out "one," "two," etc. When the leader gets to "six," time is stopped. After some discussion, the group tries to better its record with another attempt.

Language Arts:

A "part of speech" word is written on each balloon with a permanent marker. The students don't know what the word is until after they select a balloon. Five buckets are placed randomly around playing area. On the start cue, students are instructed to put the balloon in the correct bucket labeled with the appropriate part of speech; that is, nouns all end up in the noun bucket, etc.

Social Studies:

Use jump ropes or clothesline ropes to create "nets" to volley balloons over. Place students into groups of six. Two will be the enders; rotate students in accordingly. One color balloon represents Yankees; one color balloon represents Confederates. The balloons go back and forth over the Mason-Dixon Line, which is the rope.

Health:

Each color balloon represents a fruit or vegetable. Challenge participants to keep all balloons (1+ per person) in the air. This gets the group moving and cooperating. Once they have the hang of it, make it harder by adding in more balloons or placing restrictions, such as no hands, to keep balloons up. Ask participants to keep juggling the balloons but to sort them into the same fruits and veggies (works best with large groups).

FIT4LEARNING DYNA-BAND ROUTINES

Why Are We Doing This? To reinforce multiple content standards Grades K–5

What Stuff Do We Need? Fit4Learning 4-foot Dyna-Bands, Fit4Learning academic integration music

How Do We Play?

Just keep moving to the Dyna-Band exercise routines.

- Chest and triceps
- Shoulders
- Biceps
- Upper back

- Quads and hams
- Calves
- Outer thighs

Can use rubber bands

Math:

Multiplication, Division, Addition, or Subtraction Music

Science:

Singin' Science I and II

Language Arts:

Reading Readiness, Learning Language, Rockin' Reading Readiness

Social Studies:

President's Rap, American Heroes I and II

Health:

Healthy Habits

FIT4LEARNING JUGGLING ROUTINES

Why Are We Doing This? To reinforce multiple content standards Grades K–5

What Stuff Do We Need? Fit4Learning juggling scarves and Fit4Learning academic integration music

How Do We Play? Toss one scarf up in the air; catch it on top. As time goes on add another scarf, then make it three. Remember this sequence: criss-cross applesauce. Children love scarves!

The following is great music for jugglers as well as Dyna-Bands.

Math:

Multiplication, Division, Addition, or Subtraction Music

Science:

Singin' Science I and II

Language Arts:

Reading Readiness, Learning Language, Rockin' Reading Readiness

Social Studies:

President's Rap, American Heroes I and II

Health:

Healthy Habits

LET'S WRAP IT UP

As school budgets tighten and teachers have more on their plates, why not integrate multiple contents under the same template of the game? Teachers do not need to leave their core content–specific areas. In fact, step it up by adding active learning subject-matter template games for better retention and healthier kids. And integrate the Fit4Learning A.C.T.I.V.E. Standards into each lesson. Not only will your students be more active learners, they will remember the material through multiple modalities. Let's go!

6

Physical Education for Classroom Teachers

The first step to becoming is to will it.

—Mother Teresa

LET'S BEGIN

Let's wake up learning and bring the classroom alive with an abundance of fun games that no child can resist. Think back when you were a kid; playing games and interacting with the class was a whole lot more fun than just sitting there. When integrating subject-matter content into the game being played, retention of the material goes through the roof. More neural connections in the brain are made as learning is occurring through different modalities and pathways. With regard to aerobic (with oxygen) activity, the research is clear; aerobic activity prepares the brain for optimal learning.

[handwritten annotation: Importance when making master schedules!! recess.]

91

CHECK THIS OUT

In Denver, Colorado, at Conrad Middle School, Miss Snyder is up and at 'em before any other teacher on campus. One could easily say that she definitely operates on the premise "The early bird catches the worm!" After 31 years of teaching, Miss Snyder has earned the deserved reputation as "most prepared" as she takes her planning seriously and utilizes her time wisely.

Miss Snyder loves teaching. However; during the last couple of years, her teaching assignment at her middle school has changed. It requires that all of the sixth-grade classroom teachers teach the physical education (PE) classes, because PE instructors are only hired for the seventh grade and up. The sixth-grade teachers are responsible for this extra prep because of budget cuts. Yikes! On top of everything else needed to be taught, now this!

Miss Snyder hates PE. When she was a kid, she was threatened, belittled, and "put down" in PE. One could say that her memories of PE are borderline traumatic. With that kind of mistreatment, it's a "no-brainer" why she hates PE. And now she has to teach it? Ugh.

However, to her and everyone else's amazement, she not only did a great job at this addition to her day, she actually enjoyed it! She taught PE the way she wished it would have been taught to her. The students participated in activities that promoted cooperation, that anchored academic concepts, that worked on aerobic fitness, and that were fun!

Because of the cold weather conditions in Colorado, many students would beg their parents for that all important PE excuse to "get out of it." Miss Snyder wised up to these notes in a hurry, and it took quite a bit to "pull the wool over her eyes." Miss Snyder acquired quite a collection of "PE notes." In fact, they were such a hit, she collected them and kept a PE journal of her memoirs. Lucky you, here they are:

- My son is under a doctor's care and should not take PE today. Please execute him.
- Please excuse Lisa for being absent. She was sick and I had her shot.
- Dear School: Please ekscuse John being absent on Jan. 28, 29, 30, 31, 32, and also 33.
- Please excuse Gloria from Jim today. She is administrating.
- Please excuse Roland from PE for a few days. Yesterday he fell out of a tree and misplaced his hip.
- John has been absent because he had two teeth taken out of his face.
- Carlos was absent yesterday because he was playing football. He was hurt in the growing part.
- Megan could not come to school today because she has been bothered by very close veins.
- Chris will not be in school cus he has an acre in his side.
- Please excuse Ray Friday from school. He has very loose vowels.

- Please excuse Pedro from being absent yesterday. He had (diahre) (dyrea) (direathe) the shits. [Words in parentheses were crossed out.]
- Please excuse Tommy for being absent yesterday. He had diarrhea and his boots leak.
- Irving was absent yesterday because he missed his bust.
- Please excuse Jimmy for being. It was his father's fault.
- I kept Billie home because she had to go Christmas shopping because I don't know what size she wear.
- Please excuse Jennifer for missing school yesterday. We forgot to get the Sunday paper off the porch, and when we found it Monday, we thought it was Sunday.
- Sally won't be in school a week from Friday. We have to attend her funeral.
- My daughter was absent yesterday because she was tired. She spent a weekend with the Marines.
- Please excuse Jason for being absent yesterday. He had a cold and could not breed well.
- Please excuse Mary for being absent yesterday. She was in bed with gramps.
- Gloria was absent yesterday as she was having a gangover.
- Please excuse Burma, she has been sick and under the doctor.
- Please excuse little Jimmy for not being in school yesterday. His father is gone and I could not get him ready because I was in bed with the doctor.

Can you believe these notes? As you can see, it is never a dull moment in the PE world. Whether you are required to teach PE or are monitoring recess, turn into an Action-Packed experience. This is your chance to take that all important "super-movement" time and utilize it to your "academic teachers'" benefit. PE or aerobic recess may just turn out to surprise you, like Miss Snyder, and be one of your favorite hours of the day.

WHY EVEN BOTHER?

The purpose of teaching PE is because it's the law! Depending on what state or country you live in and teach in, the requirements vary. But all in all, so many minutes need to be focused on educating the physical. Because of the focus on academic testing, many schools just don't fit it into the day as (1) there's "just no time for it," (2) it's not on a top priority, and (3) it's not on the state test!

In addition to PE, time is needed for breaks from the academic curriculum, whereas the usual routine for breaks in schools is the infamous recess. Why not turn recess into a beneficial "aerobic brain" time? Why not turn the endless games of "dodgeball" at your school into a wide variety of awesome activities? And doesn't it make sense to "get the ants out of their pants" so when they arrive back in the classroom, they are focused and ready to learn? Works for me.

"Aerobic Brains" and Academics

The neuroscience research is clear. Research from all over the world has shown that exercise impacts cognition. Exercise does affect how our kids learn! The following is an example of a study conducted with mice in laboratories. Remember, all science starts with those critters before a human being is tested. All indications point to more exciting news down the line.

Of course, this is written in weird, wild, science lingo and is hard to understand. But, don't worry, it will be broken down in layman's terms after you read this (Molteni et al., 2004):

> **Exercise** reverses the harmful effects of consumption of a high-fat diet on synaptic and behavioral plasticity associated to the action of brain-derived neurotrophic factor. A diet high in total fat reduces hippocampal levels of brain-derived neurotrophic factor (BDNF), a crucial modulator of synaptic plasticity, and a predictor of learning efficacy. They evaluated the capacity of voluntary exercise to interact with the effects of diet at the molecular level. Animal groups were exposed to the high fat diet for 2 months with and without access to voluntary wheel running. **Exercise** reversed the decrease in BDNF and its downstream effectors on plasticity. In addition, exercise prevented the deficit in spatial learning induced by the diet, tested in the Morris water maze. Furthermore, levels of reactive oxygen species increased by the effects of the diet were decreased by exercise. Results indicate that exercise interacts with the same molecular systems disrupted by the high fat diet, reversing their effects on neural function. Reactive oxygen species, and BDNF in conjunction with its downstream effectors on synaptic and neuronal plasticity, are common molecular targets for the action of the diet and **exercise**. Results unveil a possible molecular mechanism by which lifestyle factors can interact at a molecular level, and provide information for potential therapeutic applications to decrease the risk imposed by certain lifestyles.

Okay, so what does this say? Bottom line, a high-fat diet reduces the "good stuff" in our brains that nourish neurons (our brain cells). Voluntary exercise reversed the damaging effects of a high-fat diet. Wow!

The key here is "voluntary" exercise. Mice love to run. But we are not mice; we are human beings. What about us? Do humans love to run? Some do, most don't, especially if it is treated as punishment or not pleasurable. And most kids have been in classes or at schools where "running laps" was the norm for the day. Most hate it! But what if there was some other form of aerobic activity that was deemed very fun and kids loved to do it? *Action-Packed Classrooms* to the rescue!

In this chapter are super games that disguise the "aerobic" beauty of exercise because they are just so much fun. When kids are having fun, they can go all day. For example, in the outdoor/field game section of this chapter, there is a game called "Crows and Cranes." Basically, this is a game where kids run 50-yard dashes for the entire class time without realizing it because the sprints are hiding behind the fun of the game. After a period of this game, your kids will be aerobically ready for academics.

So much of the research talks about more oxygen to the brain, more neuro-transmitters, more efficiency of chemicals in brain, and more. It is imperative that more of a priority is put on this very often overlooked part of the academic day.

I urge every educator, administrator, politician, and parent to read Dr. John Ratey's new book *Spark: The Revolutionary New Science of Exercise and the Brain* (2008). Dr. Ratey takes you on a fascinating journey through the mind-body connection, presenting startling new research to prove that exercise is truly the best defense against mood disorders, attention deficit hyperactivity disorder, and other behavior disorders that affect learning. Simply go to www.fit4learning.com or www.johnratey.com to get this must-read book.

The journey to create aerobic brains begins now.

EQUIPMENT AND FACILITIES ADAPTATIONS

Many questions come to mind when thinking about what it takes to do an activity that is more aerobically inclined versus inside the four walls of the academic classroom. Here is a "fright" list from a fellow teacher:

- No place to go
- No room for equipment to store in my classroom
- Don't know what to do with the equipment
- Not athletically inclined
- Not comfortable in this arena
- Don't have any equipment
- Don't have any facilities
- Little space to move

Don't worry. When perusing through the activities, games, and active fun, you will see that most activities don't use equipment and can be played virtually anywhere. The key here is to adapt. Whatever works. Every school and every campus is different. The most important objectives are (1) to get those kids moving and (2) to make sure they are safe.

The following are examples of substituting equipment:

- Socks for football flags
- Paper cups for cones
- Paper plates for poly spots

Whenever reviewing and planning an activity, think to yourself, "What can I do to substitute for equipment if I don't have what is required? How can I modify and make this game work for me and my students?" Once you have that attitude, anything and any game is possible.

Remember, it is assumed that music is included. The activities do not tell you to get a boom box for equipment and some music. Whenever you can, include it! It adds so much to any activity.

READY, SET, ACTION!

Activities for Warm-Ups

PEOPLE-TO-PEOPLE

What Stuff Do We Need? Nothing

How Do We Play?

Each student stands back to back with a partner. Teacher calls body parts and students respond by touching partner as teacher calls it (elbow to knee, foot to head, side to side, hand to quadriceps, bicep to toe, etc.). The students are laughing so hard that they are comfortable with the activity and don't realize they are touching anyone else. On the signal "people-to-people," new partners must be formed. Make sure the students solve the problems of getting a partner quickly. Group discussion on this process is part of the lesson.

TO THE RESCUE

What Stuff Do We Need? Beanbags/objects

How Do We Play?

All students have a bean bag that they put on their head in personal space. Students then GENTLY KNUDGE fellow classmates, trying to bump beanbag off of the head. If beanbag falls off, students cannot touch their own bean bag. Another student needs to come "to the rescue" and put the beanbag on their head.

ROADWAY

What Stuff Do We Need? Nothing

How Do We Play?

Students partner up back to back in general space. One partner then stands behind the other. Front partner is the "car," who places his or her hands in front of them as bumpers and closes their eyes. Back partner is the "driver," who places their hands on the partner's shoulders. On "go," they scramble egg across the general space. The driver guides the car safely (without bumping any others) by gently turning the partner's shoulders in the direction in which he or she must go to avoid a collision. Teacher says switch.

Variations: combine cars to make mini vans, combine mini vans to make limos, etc. Group discussion should be centered around trust.

BRING IT TO ME . . .

What Stuff Do We Need? Nothing

How Do We Play?

- Groups of four
- Number 1–4
- When a number is called, that person comes to me
- I will then tell them to get three items; for example, earring, pencil, belt
- First person back to me wins
- Can be done with locomotor skills instead

NEURAL CONNECTIONS

What Stuff Do We Need? Blank paper or balls

How Do We Play?

- Wad up pieces of paper making a paper ball
- Start with one paper ball
- Make a throwing pattern
- Continue adding paper balls

RE-UPTAKE

What Stuff Do We Need? Blank paper

How Do We Play?

- Wad up a piece of paper into a ball
- Put ball on floor by their feet
- Music starts, move ball with feet trying to tag other people's feet
- If they tag, they shout "uptake"
- Each person responsible for own ball

NEURAL EXPLOSION

What Stuff Do We Need? Blank paper

How Do We Play?

- Wad up a piece of paper into a ball
- Don't touch popcorn while oil heats up
- When given "synapse" cue, all players pick up balls throwing toward ceiling
- Each player yells "synapse" on each toss
- After each "synapse," move on to another ball

AXONS/DENDRITES

What Stuff Do We Need? Nothing

How Do We Play?

- People either axons or dendrites
- Music starts, move around room
- Shout out what you are
- If you meet up with the opposite, high five
- Make as many synapses as possible

HAND OFF

What Stuff Do We Need? Pencils and coins

How Do We Play?

- Two teams facing each other in straight lines
- Each team has six pencils (as markers) and one coin
- First person in line passes coin to next down the line
- Passes are quick with many false passes
- First person in opposite line shouts "stop" at any time
- Then that team huddles together to decide who has the coin
- If correct they get a marker; if not correct, other team gets marker
- Both teams rotate their first player
- Team with most markers wins

HAND CLAP RELAY

What Stuff Do We Need? Nothing

How Do We Play?

- Stand in circle around table
- Alternate hands
- Clap on table in a direction

- Double claps reverses direction
- If out of rhythm, pull hand out

AH-SO-KO

What Stuff Do We Need? Nothing

How Do We Play?

- People are standing in a circle
- AH = karate chop to neck (right or left)
- SO = karate chop over head (right or left)
- KO = karate chop pointing to someone across the circle

- If someone goofs (verbal or tactile), he or she gets harassed
- Play to final four

HI, HOW ARE YA? GOTTA GO

What Stuff Do We Need? Nothing

How Do We Play?

Students walk up to fellow classmates, shake their hands, look at them, and introduce themselves. Next, students can give the "way cool" introduction to their new classmates. They walk up to a classmate, shake hands regularly, then interlock the thumbs, then connect the thumbs and wave at each other. While they are doing this they say hi (with regular handshake), how are ya? (with interlocked thumbs), and gotta go (with thumbs connected waving by). Very fun intro activity.

CONGA LINE

What Stuff Do We Need? Nothing

How Do We Play?

- Front person leads movement
- Rest in line follow

- Rotate positions

okay for hallway?

WIGGLE-WADDLE RELAY

What Stuff Do We Need? Blank paper

How Do We Play?

- Divide into teams of six or so
- Each team has a piece of paper (wadded up) and one glass
- First player waddles with paper ball between knees up and back

- Once back, drop ball into glass without hands
- Next player takes ball from glass and repeats

WHICH-WAY-JOSE?

What Stuff Do We Need? Nothing

How Do We Play?

- Make square formation with entire group
- Line up in some kind of order
- Teacher turns facing another direction
- Group adjusts

SYNAPTIC CAPTAINS

What Stuff Do We Need? Nothing

How Do We Play?

- Partner up
- Who is receptor, who is neurotransmitter?
- Receptor closes eyes (no peeking)
- Neurotransmitter commands receptor to find wadded paper balls
- Neurotransmitter guides receptor to "hit the feet" of another receptor
- Once hit, reverse roles
- Neurotransmitters can protect their receptor by intercepting incoming balls but can never touch their receptors

WALK-ACROSS-BUDDIES

What Stuff Do We Need? Two hula hoops per group of six

How Do We Play?

- Divide into three subgroups of two
- Interlock hoops into legs
- Move across room and around an object, then come back
- Add more people until entire group becomes one

GOTCHA

What Stuff Do We Need? Nothing

How Do We Play?

- Circle up
- Each partner's left finger touches the other partner's right palm
- On count of three, attempt to pull finger out of one partner's grasp while trying to catch other partner's finger
- Repeat and reverse
- Repeat with arms crossed

WRIGHT FAMILY

What Stuff Do We Need? "Life with the Wright Family" story (see next page) and blank paper

How Do We Play?

Group stands in a circle, shoulder to shoulder, with one piece of blank paper wadded in a small ball. Object of the game: Every time the word "right" is heard, the group passes the ball one person to the right. Every time

the word "left" is heard, each person passes the ball one person to the left. When either right or left is heard, participants hop. The teacher reads story fast so it is full of action. This activity is truly a hoot!

"Life With the Wright Family"

One day the Wright family decided to take a vacation. The first thing they had to decide was who would be left at home since there was not enough room in the Wright family car for all of them. Mr. Wright decided that Aunt Linda Wright would be the one left at home. Of course this made Aunt Linda Wright so mad that she left the house immediately, yelling, "It will be a right cold day before I return."

The Wright family now bundled up the children, Tommy Wright, Susan Wright, Timmy Wright, and Shelly Wright and got in the car and left. Unfortunately, as they turned out of the driveway someone had left a trash can in the street, so they had to turn right around and stop the car. They told Tommy Wright to get out of the car and move the trash can so they could get going. Tommy took so long that they almost left him in the street. Once the Wright family got on the road, Mother Wright wondered if she had left the stove on. Father Wright told her not to worry … he had checked the stove and she had not left it on. As they turned right at the corner, everyone started to think about other things that they might have left undone.

No need to worry now; they were off on a right fine vacation.

When they arrived at the gas station, Father Wright put gas in the car and discovered that he had left his wallet at home. So Timmy Wright ran home to get the money that was left behind. After Timmy had left, Susan Wright started to feel sick. She left the car saying that she had to throw up. This of course got Mother Wright's attention and she left the car in a hurry. Shelly Wright wanted to watch Susan get sick, so she left the car too. Father Wright was left with Tommy Wright, who was playing a game in the backseat.

With all of this going on, Father Wright decided that this was not the right time to take a vacation, so he gathered up all of the family and left the gas station as quickly as he could. When he arrived home, he turned left into the driveway and said, "I wish the Wright family had never left the house today!"

TOSS A NAME GAME

What Stuff Do We Need? Six Koosh-type balls or wadded paper balls

How Do We Play?

Form a circle. Person steps forward one step and say his or her name. The entire group, in unison, says the name of that individual. Go around the circle. Now add a ball that is tossed to another person. To toss, call the name of the person, make eye contact, then easy toss. Receiver says thank you to whomever and says name. Add more balls and keep tossing and calling names. Finish by putting balls away. Go around and have the person step forward silently, and the group calls out the name.

BIRTHDAY LINE

What Stuff Do We Need? Nothing

How Do We Play?

Without saying a word or lip-synching, have students group in one line by the day of their birthday. The kids can flash fingers to indicate what month and day, but can't say anything. Then, bend the line to make a circle, go around the circle (and see if students remember their names) and say when their birthdays are. They should be right next to someone who has the same birthday or close … already something in common with fellow classmates!

PARTNER HANDSHAKES

What Stuff Do We Need? Nothing

How Do We Play?

Go around shaking hands introducing yourself and share one item of information about your last birthday. Next person you shake hands with, introduce yourself and share your info. Next person you meet and introduce yourself to, you also have to introduce the last person you shook hands with and his or her piece of information. Do this throughout the school year to get the kids to move, interact, and meet their classmates in a whole new light.

◆

Aerobic Tag and Chase Games

SCRAMBLED EGGS

What Stuff Do We Need? Nothing

How Do We Play?

Students get into personal space. When music starts, students move (any movement you decide) among each other without touching another human being. Have the students first walk, race-walk, run, skip, crawl, etc. This is a great activity to check out if there are any rowdies in your class who are not moving safely. Of course, positively reinforce the kids that are doing a great job, and the rowdies will usually settle down.

SAFETY TAG

What Stuff Do We Need? Nothing

How Do We Play?

All students are in personal space. Everybody is "it." Students safety tag fellow students on the knee (stress safety) to freeze them. When students are frozen, hands are at their hips. To unfreeze the frozen, free students touch frozen students' elbows gently. Very fun and active. You can add many variations to this basic tag game, such as high-fives, compliments, put-ups, etc.

PARTNER TAG

What Stuff Do We Need? Nothing

How Do We Play?

Students partner up back to back in general space. One of the partners is "it." All "its" spin around slowly 10 times while their partner is moving scrambled egg in the general space. "Its" open eyes and try to find partner to safety tag. Then partner is "it." All students must keep moving during this activity.

BLOB TAG

What Stuff Do We Need? Nothing

How Do We Play?

Students are in general space. Two students start the game as the Blobs. When they safety tag other students, they connect at the wrists. When they link up to four people, the Blob divides by two, so now there are more Blobs. All students need to keep moving.

BLIND TAG

What Stuff Do We Need? Blindfolds and fluffy balls or wadded paper balls

How Do We Play?

In pairs, one is sighted and one is not. One of the pair is "it" and carries a fluff ball to denote this. Sighted partner stands with the nonsighted partner and leads with voice commands only, no physical contact! Avoid being tagged by the nonsighted "it" with the fluff ball. After a while, switch sighted and nonsighted people. Before doing so, partners should discuss what things were done positively and what things could be changed.

TOE TAG

What Stuff Do We Need? Nothing

How Do We Play?

- Partner up back to back in general space.
- Partners face each other with arms on shoulders.
- Object of the activity is to tap the other person's toes.
- Switch partners a few times. Lots of fun!

TRIANGLE TAG

What Stuff Do We Need? Nothing

How Do We Play?

- Get into groups of four.
- Three of the members put hands on shoulders or hold hands, all facing to the center.
- The other member is "it" and chases one of the members of the triangle. The other two try to protect their person by moving.
- The "it" can't go under, over, or through the group.
- Rotate the "its" when they tag or are exhausted.

TIRE TAG

What Stuff Do We Need? Bicycle inner tubes or hula hoops and 12 yarn balls

How Do We Play?

Students partner up inside an inner tube. Six pairs are "its" and each holds on to a yarn ball. When the music starts, all inner-tubed partners run trying to get away from the "its." If they are tagged, they take the yarn balls and are now it. Your kids will be laughing so hard, it will be difficult for them to run.

HOT SWATTER

What Stuff Do We Need? Eight paper plates/Frisbees, eight foam sticks/soft objects

How Do We Play? *poly spots*

Maximum six students per group. One student is "it" and has the stick. All others form a circle three yards from a Frisbee, which is now in the center. The student who is "it" now strikes a participant on the leg and lays the stick on the Frisbee (can't throw it, must touch the Frisbee before letting go). The student that was struck races in and grabs the stick and tries to hit the "it" person before he or she can get to the vacated spot. If they miss, then they are the new "it" and strike another. If they hit them, then they have to lay the stick down and get back to the spot before they get hit again.

BONUS BALL

What Stuff Do We Need? Fifty-five tennis balls

How Do We Play? *tubes, ping pong balls*

This is a high-energy relay. Divide the class into six teams, no more than eight players per team. You'll need 55 tennis balls for this activity. Mark eight tennis balls with a "1," eight tennis balls with a "2," eight tennis balls with a "3," eight tennis balls with a "4," eight tennis balls with a "5," eight tennis balls with a "6," and seven balls with "BB" for bonus ball. Each team has a #10 can at the front of their line. (A #10 can is the container tennis balls come in, or you can use an old coffee can.) The teams line up parallel to one another at one end. All tennis balls are at the other end of the playing area. On the starting signal, the first four players run forward to find a tennis ball with their team's number on it. Once the player has found a numbered ball belonging to his or her team, he or she returns and places it in the team's #10 can. That player goes to end of line as the next player runs and tries to find a ball with the team's number. Bonus balls are "wild" and can be picked up by any team player once the team has found five or more of its numbered balls. Scoring: Score one point for the numbered team balls and two points for a bonus ball. Tell students to keep it a secret if they find a bonus ball. This makes it more exciting when totaling up scores.

◆

Inside/Playground Games

TOE JAM

What Stuff Do We Need? Paper balls

How Do We Play?

- Participants are partnered up
- Each person has a paper ball
- Partners stay connected by interlocking arms at shoulder height
- Aim for partner's feet
- Each person takes a shot before retrieving ball
- Faking moves and quick feet recommended

WHISTLE MIXER

What Stuff Do We Need? Nothing

How Do We Play?

Students are moving in scrambled egg formation. Teacher blows whistle a certain number of times, and kids get back to back depending on the number of whistles. For example, four whistles (group of four), three whistles (group of three), etc. Great activity for students to get into groups quickly. Group discussion on this process is part of lesson.

MATCH MATES

What Stuff Do We Need? Nothing

How Do We Play?

Players are in a scattered formation. When the music starts, the students begin walking around in the general space. When the music stops, the players freeze and listen to the leader, who tells how the groups will be formed. For example, "Show us how quickly you can form groups by the color of your eyes." After the group is formed, players greet each other. Players repeat the activity, performing other locomotor movements (running, skipping, jumping) and using other criterion for group formation (birthday month, first vowel in last name, color of shoes, etc.).

UNTOUCHABLES

What Stuff Do We Need? Hula hoop

How Do We Play?

- Make square formation with entire group
- Opposite sides walk across without touching anyone

- Add hoop in center as obstacle
- Time the groups for challenge

[handwritten annotation: Can not square from square from Do during restroom break]

HOG CALL

What Stuff Do We Need? Blindfolds

How Do We Play?

Partners create names that match, such as peanut & butter, salt & pepper, black & white, etc. One partner is one name, one partner is the other. Partners must split into two groups about 30 yards apart. Everyone blindfolds themselves. Teacher says go, and all students call out their partners' matching name.

BRAINY BARNYARD

What Stuff Do We Need? Blindfolds

How Do We Play?

Same as Hog Call, except students are scattered in general space. Students have a choice of either being a sheep, cow, horse, pig, dog, or rooster (any animals you choose) but decide what they are going to be secretly. Once students are blindfolded, the teacher says go, and all students act out what they are (i.e., cow goes moo). Students should end up in groups of the same animals.

KNOTS

What Stuff Do We Need? Nothing

How Do We Play?

Students get in groups of eight. Join hands with two different people across the circle. After all students have joined hands, try to undo your giant knot without letting go. Have the kids try it a couple times in their groups, then combine groups.

NEURAL TRANSMITTERS

What Stuff Do We Need? PVC pipes cut into 18-inch pieces cut lengthwise (make a trough), six marbles, and 12 cones

How Do We Play?

- Object of game: transport neural message (marble) along neural pathway (PVC pipes) from one receptor site to another (the cones)
- Can't touch message (marble)

- Can't walk with PVC pipe
- If message falls on ground, start over
- Receptor site can't be moved

SKIN THE SNAKE

What Stuff Do We Need? Nothing

How Do We Play?

Divide the class into teams of six. Have each team find a space and get into file formation behind a leader. Be sure the kids have enough space. Emphasize that players keep their legs in close while lying down. Remind players to keep the hand hold at all times. Warn players to walk with legs wide apart to avoid treading on their teammates. Object of game: Spread your legs apart, lean over, put your right hand forward to grasp the hand of the player in front to you; then, put your left hand back between your legs to grasp the extended hand of the player behind you. Hold the hands of both players throughout the game. On the signal "Go," the last player lies down as the rest of the team backs up over him, straddling him with legs apart. Then each player in turn lies down for the team to shuffle backward over you until everyone is lying down, still holding hands. The last player (first to lie down) gets to his feet, then straddle walks forward over the rest of the team, pulling each one in turn to the standing position until everyone is back in the original position. This activity really works on flexibility but definitely is best when the boys and girls are separated.

JUMP ROPE CHALLENGES

What Stuff Do We Need? One giant rope and lots of single ropes

How Do We Play?

Giant Rope. Two students take the rope by its ends and begin turning. The rest of the students will be jumpers, lining up single file. The students proceed to pass through the turning rope. Explain to the class how to judge timing so that they jump in when the rope is at its highest point and how to jump out. Change the rope turners when needed. Challenge students to go through the turning rope, then two by two, four by four, eight by eight, etc., until entire class goes through the rope.

Station Cards. Use jump rope station cards to teach different jump skills to music. For example, one station might instruct students to jump on their right foot. Other stations would have them jump on the left foot, jump rope backward, criss-cross their arms as they jump, etc. I always introduce this as the best conditioner for athletics to eliminate any student referring to jumping rope as something for sissies.

[handwritten notes in top margin]

FOUR SQUARE

What Stuff Do We Need? Playground balls and squares on floor

How Do We Play?

Introduce this game as "Middle School" four square, which is nothing like the game they played in elementary school! Or you can keep it low key for the younger ones—whatever your choice. This is very fast paced, which requires a lot of agility and quick reaction time. The students must keep their fingers pointed down. If the ball bounces on the line, the student is out (but still a winner). The server must say, "Service." Students really enjoy this game.

PUSH-UP WAVE

What Stuff Do We Need? Nothing

How Do We Play?

Have the entire class form a large circle holding hands. When a circle has been created, drop hands. All students get in push-up starting position while in the circular formation. Designate one student to be the starting person. On the signal to start, the students hold themselves about one inch off the ground in a push-up position. Everyone goes down in a "wave" order. When the "wave" comes around again the students push themselves back up to the starting position. Challenge the class to see how many times they can do the "push-up wave!"

GROUP JUGGLING

What Stuff Do We Need? Koosh-type balls

How Do We Play?

Group of six or eight students form a circle. Provide one fewer ball than the number of members in the group. The leader has all of the balls at his or her feet. Toss one ball gently to someone across the circle. Keep tossing the one ball across the circle to anyone who hasn't received the ball. Remember who you tossed to and who tossed to you. Once you have a pattern that includes everyone in your group, add more equipment.

◆

Outside/Field Games

TWO-DEEP FITNESS

What Stuff Do We Need? Twenty cones/objects

How Do We Play?

Set up the cones to create two circles, one small circle inside a big circle. Students are in groups of two. One partner is in the outside circle with his or her partner standing in front of him or her in the inside circle. There is a leader in the middle. The inside circle follows the movements of the leader who creates any kind of movement, such as push-ups. At the same time, the outside circle jogs one lap around the outside circle of cones, without passing another student. Once students get back to their partners, they stop, jogging in place. On the signal to switch, partners switch places. Now there is a new inside circle following the leader's movements and a new outside circle jogging! Continue the activity.

SHARK ATTACK

What Stuff Do We Need? Parachute (or sheet), life vests (adapt), and *Jaws* theme song

How Do We Play?

This game is a hoot!

- Object of game: to not get eaten by the sharks and pulled under the parachute
- One shark on hands and knees under parachute

- People sit down holding parachute
- Play *Jaws* music
- Shark tugs at people
- Lifeguard saves beachgoers

CROWS AND CRANES

What Stuff Do We Need? Football flags/clothespins

Game from Rugby guys?

How Do We Play?

Super fun game. "Grow this up" for middle school by talking about the center line as the "line of scrimmage," or just tell the younger kids to line up on a line. Students are about a foot off the center line facing each other (yellow flags, "crows," on one side; red flags, "cranes," on the other). There are end boundaries about 50 or so feet from the center line. Object of the game is not to get points. Teacher says, "Croooooooowwwwwwssss" and yellow flagged "crows" run to the end zone as fast as they can before the cranes pull their flags. Teacher says, "Crrrrraaaaaannnnnneeessss" and red flagged "cranes" run to the end zone as fast as they can before the crows pull their flags. If a flag is pulled, put it back on, and you now have a point. I say, "Bak, bak, bak," like a chicken when the kids don't want to go up to the line of scrimmage—they love it! Variations include integrating subject matter into the activity. Instead of crows or cranes, the groups could be "odd" or "even" numbers. The teacher calls out, for example, "Nine times five equals?" If the answer is odd, the odd group chases the even group and vice versa. The groups could be "nouns" or "verbs." Be creative.

ROCK, PAPER, SCISSORS

What Stuff Do We Need? Football flags/clothespins

How Do We Play?

Same as Crows and Cranes except students get a partner facing them across the scrimmage line (doesn't matter what color flag). Teacher says, "Ready, set, go." Students then rock, paper, scissors. Whoever wins that round chases, and the other student gets chased. It's fun to watch the kids process this info quickly.

BRITISH BULLDOG

What Stuff Do We Need? Football flags/clothespins

How Do We Play?

Mark out the play area with a safe zone at each end. Select one player to be "it" who stands in the middle of the play area. Have all other players wear flags. When the teacher shouts through a megaphone, "British Bulldog, 1, 2, 3!" all players try to run to the safe zone at the opposite end of the play area before the "it" player can pull their flag. Tagged players become "its" and join the other Bulldogs in the middle of the play area. Flags should be returned to the teacher. Students may change ends only when the "British Bulldog" signal is called. Now, teacher repeats, "British Bulldog, 1, 2, 3!" and players again try to run to the opposite safe zone. Continue until there are more Bulldogs than runners. Stress safety in this game and the importance of watching where you are going. It is suggested that spinning is not allowed.

DOG AND A BONE

What Stuff Do We Need? Ten towel strips, each tied in a knot

How Do We Play?

Form equal teams of six players. Have the teams line up behind the opposite end lines, about 10 meters (30 feet) apart, facing each other. Number the players in each line, 1, 2, 3, 4, 5, and 6, with the number 1's at opposite ends. Place a "bone" (towel) midway between the two lines. When the teacher calls a number (for example, 2) both number 2's leap forward and attempt to snatch the bone and return to their home line, without being tagged by their opponent. If successful, they earn one point for their team. If their opponent tags them, the tagger's team gets the point. Players may trick and jockey for a position before making the snatch for the towel. One player needs to keep score for their team. Continue until each player's number has been called at least once. Have five or six games going on at once.

ROCKS

What Stuff Do We Need? Thirty Frisbees/paper plates, two large hoops, jerseys (adapt), 20 cones/objects

How Do We Play?

Object of the game is to capture opponent's rocks while protecting your own. Game starts with a whistle. Players are "safe" on their own side of the field. Once they cross into opponent's field, they are liable to be safety tagged. Inside hoop is safe. If tagged, player must "freeze" by putting hands on hips. A teammate can be "unfrozen" by a player tapping elbows. The unfrozen player must check in across the midline to his or her side before doing anything else (going to rock pile or unfreezing anyone else). Players will try to get into opponent's circle, grab a rock, and return to their own circle without being tagged. If a player is tagged with a rock in hand, the tagged player will give the rock to the other team and go back to his or her home side (he or she is not frozen). One foot over the center line or one foot into the hoop and a player is safe. The players guarding the rock pile must stay six feet from the rock pile. The game is over when one team has all the rocks in their circle. Encourage students to take risks, rescue teammates, and play honest! After a few games, the students come up with some very interesting strategies.

TENNIS BALL RELAY

What Stuff Do We Need? Twenty tennis balls

How Do We Play?

The tennis ball relay is an activity designed to give students a great aerobic workout in an enjoyable atmosphere. A cone is needed as a starting point for each three-person team. Everyone in class is on a three-person team. The teams should be made up or picked so that each team has a balance. To start the race, place two players from each team at their starting marker with the tennis ball on the ground in front of the first player.

Place the third player on the team at the far end of the field. Instruct the students that when the race starts, the first player on the team is to kick the tennis ball "soccer style" so that the ball flies to the end of the field. The person who kicked the ball chases it. When he or she arrives at the other end of the field, his or her teammate kicks the ball back to the player who remained at the starting point. This player, in turn, when the ball gets there, kicks it all the way back to runner number 1 who is waiting at the far end of the field. The runners continue this pattern for 10 minutes or so, counting how many times they completed a cycle.

PASS THE SHOE

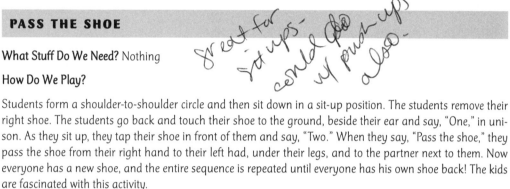

great for sit ups – could do with push-ups also –

What Stuff Do We Need? Nothing

How Do We Play?

Students form a shoulder-to-shoulder circle and then sit down in a sit-up position. The students remove their right shoe. The students go back and touch their shoe to the ground, beside their ear and say, "One," in unison. As they sit up, they tap their shoe in front of them and say, "Two." When they say, "Pass the shoe," they pass the shoe from their right hand to their left had, under their legs, and to the partner next to them. Now everyone has a new shoe, and the entire sequence is repeated until everyone has his own shoe back! The kids are fascinated with this activity.

SWEDISH SOFTBALL

What Stuff Do We Need? Two tennis rackets, two bats, two foxtails (ball in sock), objects used for bases, and two tennis balls

How Do We Play?

Set up two softball playing areas so two games can be going on at once. Divide your class into four teams. Teams or players do not pitch to each other. Each batter throws up the tennis ball or foxtail and hits it himself or herself. After the player hits the ball, he or she is to run the bases as far as possible before the ball reaches the pitcher's hand. If a runner is between bases when the ball reaches the pitcher's hand, that player must return to first base. There are no outs. And, if a runner doesn't think he or she can make it to the next base, that player can stay put. There can be many runners on one base at a time. A team is a bat until all players on that team have batted. They then take the field and the other team bats. The running team scores by running past home plate. Runners who have scored get a free trip back to first (they keep going around the bases). The team in the field can score, too. They are awarded a point when they catch a batted ball on the fly and when they catch a runner or runners between bases by getting the ball back to the pitcher's hand. Runners on the team at bat run the bases until their team takes the field. Fielders throw "whatever" was used to all fielders before throwing to pitcher. Not sure why this game is called Swedish Softball, but it's sure to be a lot of fun!

INNER TUBE/HULA HOOP RELAY

What Stuff Do We Need? Bicycle inner tubes

How Do We Play?

Divide class into teams of four students. Divide each four-person team into pairs. Send one pair to the start/finish line, the other pair 40–60 feet away. The first person at the start line runs to the teammates at the opposite end, holding on to the inner tube. One teammate joins with the first person, holding on to the tube. The two of them run back toward the start/finish line to pick up the third teammate. The three friends, all holding on, run back to pick up the fourth friend. All four return to the start/finish line, running together, all holding on. Try groups of 8. Or 16. Or the whole class!!!

THROW AND RUN

What Stuff Do We Need? Thirty-two cones/objects and soft balls

How Do We Play?

Very modified softball-type game without bats or bases. Set up a hitting cone, running cone, and side boundary cones for a skinny field with no end boundaries. At least six players per playing area. If you had 48 students in your class, set up eight fields of six players. Positions are catcher, thrower, pitcher, and the rest are fielders. Pitcher tosses ball underhand to batter, who catches it. Batter then can throw the ball anywhere in fair territory. Batter's goal is to run around the boundary cones and get back to home base before the ball does. The ball must be thrown to all of the fielders before throwing it home. The fielders need to set up a relay system to get the ball to all players quickly. Players then rotate one position clockwise so that all players get equal chances to play all positions.

TRIANGLE SOCCER

What Stuff Do We Need? Soccer balls and cones/objects

How Do We Play?

One soccer ball and three cone markers per group. Use groups of four players. Three players form a triangle and pass the ball around from player to player. Use cones to mark the triangle formation. As the ball is passed to another player, all three players move one space clockwise. The fourth player will try to intercept the ball. The players should try and move to an open place to receive the passed ball. Rotate players throughout the drill so that everyone gets to play defense.

SOCCER CROQUET

What Stuff Do We Need? Soccer balls, coat hangers for wickets, and goals

How Do We Play?

Using the coat hanger wickets, design a gate for the soccer ball to pass through. Number the gates and follow in order the numbers 1 to 9. Have about 30 feet between numbered wickets to help give players enough room to play unhindered. After completing all wickets, the player gets to dribble for a goal shot. Arrange players at different wickets to start the activity.

ROUNDERS

What Stuff Do We Need? Two soccer balls, cones/objects, and bases (adapt)

How Do We Play?

Set up two softball playing areas so two games can be going on at once. Divide your class into four teams. Teams or players do not pitch to each other. Each batter kicks the soccer ball himself or herself. After the player kicks the ball, he or she is to run the bases as far as possible before the ball reaches the pitcher's hand. If a runner is between bases when the ball reaches the pitcher's hand, that player must return to first base. There are no outs. And, if a runner doesn't think he or she can make it to the next base, that player can stay put. There can be many runners on one base at a time. A team is "up" until all players on that team have kicked. They then take the field and the other team kicks. The running team scores by running past home plate. Runners who have scored get a free trip back to first (they keep going around the bases). The team in the field can score, too. They are awarded a point when they catch a kicked ball on the fly and when they catch a runner or runners between bases by getting the ball back to the pitcher's hand. Runners on the team at bat run the bases until their team takes the field. It's okay if it gets a little crowded on a base. At least you can have more students at one time experience running bases instead of the usual, three strikes your out. In that scenario, many times a student won't get to run a base at all!

KICK AND RUN

What Stuff Do We Need? Thirty-two cones/object and soccer balls

How Do We Play?

Very modified soccer game. Set up a kicking cone, running cone, and side boundary cones for a skinny field with no end boundaries. Positions are catcher, kicker, pitcher, and the rest are fielders. Under hand toss by pitcher to kicker, who catches the ball. Kicker then can kick the ball anywhere in fair territory. Kicker's goal is to dribble another soccer ball around the running cone and back to home base before the ball makes it back. The ball must be kicked to all of the fielders before kicking it home. The fielders need to set up a relay system to get the ball to all players quickly. Players then rotate one position clockwise so that all players get equal chances to play all positions.

TRIANGLE HOCKEY

What Stuff Do We Need? Hockey sticks, balls, and cones/objects

How Do We Play?

One hockey ball and three cone markers per group. Use groups of four players. Three players form a triangle and pass the ball around from player to player. Use cones to mark the triangle formation. As the ball is passed to another player, all three players move one space clockwise. The fourth player will try and intercept the ball. The players should try and move to an open place to receive the passed ball. Rotate players throughout the drill so that everyone gets to play defense.

HIT AND RUN

What Stuff Do We Need? Thirty-two cones/objects, eight tennis racquets, and eight tennis balls

How Do We Play?

Very modified hitting game. Set up a hitting cone, running cone, and side boundary cones for a skinny field with no end boundaries. Positions are catcher, kicker, pitcher, and the rest are fielders. Underhand toss by pitcher to hitter, who catches the ball. Hitter then can hit the ball anywhere in fair territory. Hitter's goal is to run around the boundary cones and back to home base before the ball makes it back. The ball must be thrown to all of the fielders and pitcher and before throwing it to the catcher. The fielders need to set up a relay system to get the ball to all players quickly. Players then rotate one position clockwise so that all players get equal chances to play all positions.

BIG BALL THROW

What Stuff Do We Need? Giant ball, 50 yarn balls

How Do We Play?

Put a giant ball in the center of the playing area. There are two teams on each side of the area (they must stay on their own side), or you may have four teams (put ball at the intersection of four squares). Each team has two retrievers that may go anywhere in playing area. The retrievers return the balls to the players. Object of the game: For the teams behind the lines to throw yarn balls at the giant ball and have it pass over the other teams playing area. If the retriever gets hit with the large ball, that team gets one point (you don't want any points). Repeat. Super fun stuff!

Special Favorites: Basketball and Water Fun

ZONE PASSING BASKETBALL

What Stuff Do We Need? Basketballs, jerseys (adapt), and cones/objects

How Do We Play?

This is a great way to teach passing. The court is separated into four zones. Number the zones #1, #2, #3, and #4 and mark off with cones. Divide teams into groups of nine, or 18 per court. Three students are in each zone, alternating zones. For example, team A will start three people per zone #1, three people per zone #3, and three people behind an end line not adjacent to their team. Team B will start three people per zone #2, three people per zone #4, and three people behind an end line not adjacent to their team. The game begins with a center jump. The ball then must be played by passing (chest, bounce, or overhead) from one zone to the next. Players cannot leave their zone. A score is made when an end zone player catches a pass beyond the end line. After a score, or following a dropped end-line pass, the opposing team gains possession in its nearest zone. The ball cannot be dribbled, held for more than five seconds, or passed over two zones. Passing within the same zone is allowed. Players should be rotated from zone to zone every four to five minutes.

GOAL BALL

What Stuff Do We Need? Basketballs and jerseys (adapt)

How Do We Play?

This lead-up game involves dribbling and passing. The object is to score by passing the basketball to a teammate inside one of the team's two goal areas taped in the four corners of the basketball court. The game begins with either a center jump or by one team inbounding the ball at the X. The players move the ball down the court to score by combining dribbling and passing. A goal is scored when a teammate in the goal box catches a passed ball in flight. Opponents attempt to prevent a score by guarding players but cannot enter the goal box. A ball going out of bounds is awarded to the opponents for a throw in at that spot. After a goal, the opposing team puts the ball in play at the X. If a violation occurs, the ball is awarded to the offended team for a throw in. The following constitute violations: traveling, contacting an opponent (foul), bouncing the ball to the teammate in the goal, stepping into the opponent's goal. The game is designed for 10 players. The players can be allowed to play full court or separated into an offensive and a defensive team, which must remain on their half of the court. One modification of the game is to have no one assigned to the goal areas. Therefore, any player may enter the box at any time to receive a scoring pass.

SIDELINE BASKETBALL

What Stuff Do We Need? Basketballs and jerseys (adapt)

How Do We Play?

This is another great lead-up game that involves passing and shooting. This is a participation activity that can be played with 16 students per court (eight players per team). The teams are positioned so that half of each team is on the court at one time, the other half is positioned along the sidelines. The number on the playing court is four players per team. These players can move from end to end or be restricted to half-court play. The game begins with a center jump. Scoring and fouls are the same as in basketball. When the defensive team obtains possession of the ball, they must pass it to at least one sideline player before it can be shot. The sideline player cannot shoot the ball, but only pass it to an on-court teammate. After a basket or three to four minutes of play, the on-court and sideline players exchange places. The game can be modified by allowing on-court players to dribble by requiring more than one sideline pass before a shot is taken, etc.

BASKET BOWL

What Stuff Do We Need? Playground balls (adapt) and tubs

How Do We Play?

This game is a cross between basketball and hockey, with a hockey goal (tub) at each end of the court and small utility balls for equipment. The players dribble and pass the balls as is done in basketball except for one major difference; more than one ball, and as many as five, may be in play simultaneously. This tactic really speeds up the game and spreads the players out across the court rather than crowded around one player with the ball. In this game, as in basketball, no contact is allowed. Object of the game: To score as many points as possible by throwing the balls into the goal protected by a goalie, who considers the area his or her private domain. The goalie's job is much more challenging because his or her attention is divided among the many balls coming toward the goal. This game can be played on a basketball court with the free-throw lane as the goal area or on an open field, which encourages passing the ball rather than dribbling. It is highly recommended that the goalie wears eye protection because of the many balls in play coming from all directions.

KICK-BALL BASKETBALL

What Stuff Do We Need? Rubber playground ball and jerseys (adapt)

How Do We Play?

Six students on each team. One team is up to kick. One corner of the court is home, one corner is first, one corner is second, and one corner is third. Out "court" team has a pitcher, who rolls the ball to first player up; that player kicks the ball and runs the bases (or corners). The out "court" team passes to everyone on team and has to make a basket before runner gets home. Running team gets one point every time they pass home, and they keep running the bases. Out "court" team gets five points if they make a basket before the running team player who kicked the ball makes a home run. All running team players kick and then go out "court" and vice versa.

STRIKEBALL BASKETBALL

What Stuff Do We Need? Three playground balls

How Do We Play?

Six students on each team. One team is up to strike the ball. One corner of the court is home, one corner is first, one corner is second, and one corner is third. Out "court" team has a pitcher who bounces the ball to first player up, that player strikes the ball with their hand, and runs the bases (or corners). Out "court" players have to be more than 10 feet from each other. The out "court" team passes to everyone on team and has to make a basket before runner gets home. Running team gets one point every time they pass home, and they keep running the bases. Out "court" team gets five points if they make a basket before the running team player who strikes the ball makes a home run. All running team players strike and then go out "court" and vice versa.

PCV WATER RELAY

What Stuff Do We Need? Six PCV pipes, six giant tubs, six cans, at least 24 paper cups, and water

How Do We Play?

Great way to incorporate teamwork. The relay is set up with six giant tubs full of water in a row about 10 feet from each other. At the other end of each tub is a can as far away from the tub as you like. Each tub has a 1-inch diameter PCV pipe cut about 4 feet long. Each pipe has a bunch of holes drilled in it. Each tub has one paper cup. Object of the game: To transport water from tub to can via the PCV pipe. And yes, because of the holes in the pipe, water will squirt out at them. The students need to work together and plug them up so they can fill the pipe up with water. Total cooperation is needed. The cup is used to pour the water; it can't be used for the bottom of the pipe. Extra cups are for broken ones. This game is a blast.

SHEET RACES

What Stuff Do We Need? Sheets, six giant tubs of water, six cups, and six cans

How Do We Play?

Another great water game. The relay is set up with six giant tubs full of water in a row about 10 feet from each other. At the other end of each tub is a can as far away from the tub as you like. Each tub has next to it one paper cup and a sheet. Object of the game: To transport water from tub to can via a student sitting in the sheet holding the paper cup of water. The other students grab the corners of the sheet and drag the one student sitting with the water. They run down to the can. The student in the sheet pours the water into the can, gets out of the sheet, and all team members run back to the tub. Another student gets the cup full of water and sits in the sheet. Repeat until all team players have gone. Extra cups are for broken ones. This will be, by far, one of your students' favorite activities. And what a workout! The kids are exhausted by the end of the class.

"WET 'N' WILD" WATER TRANSPORT

What Stuff Do We Need? Four buckets, at least 36 paper cups, and water

How Do We Play?

Fun water game. Students are divided into two groups. Both groups sit shoulder to shoulder on grass in two lines, facing each other. The lines should be about 10 feet apart from each other. Put a bucket at all ends of the lines; each line has a full bucket of water; another one is empty. Full bucket has 12 cups sitting next to it. Object of the game: To transport water from the full bucket via the cups to the empty bucket from one student to the other. When water is poured into empty bucket, the empty cups are sent back to the full bucket by the students passing them one to the other. This is like an assembly line. Each student can only have one full cup and one empty cup in their hand at one time. There will be two things going on at once. Full cups are traveling toward the empty bucket, while the empty ones are going back. Extra cups are for broken ones. Fun, fun, fun.

WATER WATCHOUT

What Stuff Do We Need? Six tubs, six cans, at least 24 paper cups, and water

How Do We Play?

Students are divided into six groups. The relay is set up with six giant tubs full of water in a row about 10 feet from each other. At the other end of each tub is a can as far away from the tub as you like. Each tub has next to it one paper cup. Object of the game: To transport water from tub to can via a cup balanced on the head of the first student in line. Repeat until all team players have gone. Extra cups are for broken ones. Don't worry, the students are not standing around in line as this game moves faster than you think. Another fun activity.

MAKE IT HAPPEN

The "Recess/Physical Education Checklist for Aerobic Brains" (located in Resources) is a great tool to help you "make it happen" in your classroom. In the first column, you will list whatever game or activity you are doing. There may be that one activity for the lesson per criteria, or more. A, B, and C are listed so you may list multiple games under the same criteria. Columns 2 and 3 provide space to list the facilities and equipment that would be needed.

You should find this checklist a welcome addition as it provides a clear direction of what activity you are doing, where or what facility are you using, and what equipment you will need. When everything is written down on this list, then you are good to go!

LET'S WRAP IT UP

Are you motivated yet? How could you not be? With the impact of aerobic exercise on our students' brains, it's no wonder that you have this newfound awareness of the importance of high-impact movement. And with a ton of fun, easy-to-implement activities and games, why not go for it? The key is to act on this chapter now. Turn recess at your school into an "Aerobic Brain Training Ground." You can implement cooperative aerobic PE into your day and actually enjoy it thanks to these games. You are the expert at your school, so let's take charge. Giddy up, rawhide!

7

Organizing Action-Packed Academics in Standards-Based Classrooms

I dream my painting and then paint my dream.

—Vincent Van Gogh

LET'S BEGIN

Okay, clean the closet, clean my room, clean my desktop . . . enough already! Now you are telling me to get organized? Yes indeed, without having materials in a handy, good-to-go format, you will be snorkeling throughout the school year wondering where all of those great ideas are hiding. Like an artist with a blank canvas, you have a vision of where you are and where you want to go. Then, organize materials that make sense out of this journey. Not only is this process vital to your sanity as an instructor, but it is also freeing and cleansing to the overwhelming task we have to our chosen profession—teaching. Once this is accomplished, we can plan our lessons for optimal learning.

CHECK THIS OUT

Every school has one. You know, the teacher that for the life of her is completely disheveled, unorganized, upside down, and thoroughly discombobulated. The amazing thing is she seems to make it all happen and usually with flying colors. How does she do it?

Most of us are not that fortunate. We need to plan, organize, and get our stuff together, both mentally and physically. Check out this amazing story about the mind and how the "disorganization" of the letters seems to not hinder its message:

THE PAOMNNEHAL PWEOR OF THE HMUAN MNID

I cdnuolt blveiee taht I cluod aulaclty uesdnatnrd waht I was rdgnieg! Aoccdrnig to rscheearch at Cmabrigde Uinervtisy, it deosn't mttaer in waht oredr the ltteers in a wrod are, the olny iprmoatnt tihng is that the frist and lsat ltteer be in the rghit pclae. The rset can be a taotl mses and you can sitll raed it wouthit porbelm. Tihs is bcuseae the human mnid deos not raed ervey lteter by istlef, but the wrod as a wlohe. Amzanig huh?

It is *very* amazing, isn't it? The letters in the words are so mixed up, yet we still understand the paragraph's meaning and content.

However; when organizing our daily routines, lessons, and units, we are not so lucky. It is imperative that we have our "ducks in a row."

WHY EVEN BOTHER?

Are you tired of the clutter in your classroom? Do you have piles and stacks where your desktop should be? *Action-Packed Classrooms* to the rescue. In this chapter are some handy tips to help you get organized.

STRESS MANAGEMENT

Before organizing and managing materials, it is of utmost importance to manage stress levels with yourself. Teaching is not easy! You are important. The energy it takes to keep up with all of those kids is immeasurable. With all of the demands on teachers today, the stress can shoot through the roof! The following are good starts to chill before you begin any kind of planning:

- *Aerobic exercise* (be physically active at least 30 minutes a day)—I would not be able to function in this crazy world without aerobic exercise. I do it to self-regulate; fitness is a side bonus.
- *Communicate* (confide in trusted friends and colleagues)
- *Take a break!* (read a book, enjoy some exercise, go for a walk)
- *Be good to yourself* (your thoughts, time, and energies)

- *Be realistic about yourself* (being perfect is unhealthy)
- *Praise yourself* (recognize what a great teacher you are)
- *Focus on others* (be kind)

Keeping this in mind helps as you prepare for learning to occur in your students. What is one of the first things you need to think about? Is time management important? Let's take a look.

TIME MANAGEMENT

When teachers approach each school year, they usually will realize and ask themselves, "What do I do with all of this stuff?" Because "out with the old, in with the new" also applies to the calendars for lesson planning we use, it never hurts to mention again the importance of organization and daily planning, especially for you new or upcoming teachers.

The variety of calendars for daily, weekly, and monthly lesson planning indicates how people's styles of organization vary. Some people use paper organizers or computer software, but the key to any successful planning system is religious use and custom modification. Others use pocket organizers that display a week at a time for easy reference to what's coming up in the next few days and sticky notes to write important dates or information so that they can be moved as schedules change.

Some of us keep a constantly changing phone list near our phones or on our computers, and also tape trimmed copies into the inside page of our calendars. And some of us stick a small pad of sticky notes in the back of the calendar or anywhere else so that we can jot down quick notes whenever we need to.

If you are a visual person, perhaps using mind-map symbolism, graphic organizers, or flow charts will help organize the tons of lessons to be taught on your calendar. Use mind-map symbols to indicate various activities by drawing that symbol next to an item on your calendar. This may seem like overkill, but if you're the type of person who makes detailed notes in lesson planning, and especially if you're already familiar with the project management process, transferring this metaphor to your lesson planning calendar may seem like a logical and beneficial step.

Set a time, say, right after school is out each day, to review your plans, flip ahead a week or month to see what's coming up. Something to schedule religiously: make your copies a week in advance before the copy machine breaks down! How many times has that happened?

How often have you made a list of "lessons to do today" and then have only a fraction of the activities done at the end of day? One of the keys of managing lessons is to keep track of time. So do some serious prioritizing and estimating of the time needed for a given objective, then only list as many activities as you can comfortably get done within the given time frame. Otherwise, if everything's not done, it may be because you've planned 40 hours of activities to do in one day!

DEFINING STANDARDS-BASED INSTRUCTION

Sometimes it is not enough to begin and end with the definition. Embedded within its context is terminology that lends itself to further explanation, study, or review. In this case, it is necessary to look deeper into the meaning of standards-based instruction to further understand the connection with standards and assessment.

- First, placing emphasis on standards provides guidance and support to all involved constantly reflecting upon predetermined learning objectives. A precise understanding of standards and their part in the assessment process needs to be addressed. Reinforce the overall role of standards, which is to present a clear picture of what a student should know and be able to do.
- Second, it is just as essential to maintain alignment with the standard while planning instructional activities as it is to develop the assessment. The wording of the standards becomes the guidepost throughout the planning process. Keywords from the standard guide the educator and students along the most direct route toward meeting the expectations of the learning objective.
- Third, although it is true that effective instruction results in the attainment of beneficial information, realize that students must also learn how and where to apply knowledge.

Now that standards-based instruction has been well defined, it is time to examine standards-based planning. Keep in mind that standards-based instruction aligned to standards includes appropriate and meaningful activities that engage students in the learning process and incorporate higher-order thinking skills.

CREATING CLEAR LEARNING OBJECTIVES

The best place to begin is to locate the content standards you need to address. You will want to read the definitions of content and performance standards in your state. Between national, state, district and schoolwide standards, it is imperative to have this information close at hand before proceeding. You may be able to search your standards on the Internet organized by state, grade level, and content area.

Once you've found the standards you wish to address, write them down or copy them to your word processor so you'll have them available when you're ready to design your own lesson. You may wish to use the following questions as guidelines for choosing your objectives.

What type of lesson might support those standards (for example, action-based learning, direct instruction, inquiry learning, collaborative projects, etc.)?

- How does this lesson address the learning styles and needs of your students?
- What review of prerequisite skills and knowledge is necessary?

- Will your students be motivated by this lesson?
- Do they see the value and relevance of this lesson?

DESIGNING LEARNING OBJECTIVES

Don't reinvent the wheel. Has anyone else created a lesson plan similar to the one you have in mind? How can you find out? Why not adopt or adapt a lesson that already exists? Take a look at the various action-based learning tools in this book and integrate them into lessons you are already teaching, elaborating the content with movement.

Where can you find other ideas? Use a search engine such as Google, Yahoo! or any of the search engines found on the Internet, then enter a keyword such as "earth," "fractions," or "adjectives," or any topic you'd like to explore. The possibilities are endless.

Next, ask yourself these questions:

- How well is my lesson aligned with my state's content standards?
- How active and engaging is my lesson?
- How does my lesson encourage my students to take responsibility for their own learning?
- How will my students use their knowledge to solve authentic problems related to an identified real-world problem or issue?
- How do the activities promote higher-level thinking?
- How do they provide ways for my students to demonstrate their learning besides a question/answer test?

The "Standards-Based Unit Planner" in the Resources section is a tool to help you organize your lessons according to standards.

IMPLEMENTING A LESSON

For starters, locate some online resources that can support your lesson. There are jillions of websites that provide incredible information when planning. Microsoft, Apple for Education, and Discovery School are excellent resources for great ideas.

This following lesson plan template was designed to make lesson plan writing easier to do while ensuring that all lesson plan components are met. These are a few of the parts of a lesson that need to be implemented. Of course, you may have your own favorite lesson format that works for you. Terrific! This is just a reminder that these concepts have been thought about.

- Lesson Plan Title:
  - Concept/Topic to Teach:

o Standards:
o Specific Objectives:
- General Lesson:
  o Required Materials:
  o Anticipatory Set (Lead-In):
  o Action-Packed Component
  o Step-by-Step Procedure:
- Closure (Reflect Anticipatory Set):
  o Assessment Based on Objectives:
  o Adaptations (for Students With Learning Disabilities)
  o Adaptations for Little Space
  o Extensions (for Gifted Students):
  o Connections to Other Subjects

Now that our lesson plan is organized, let's organize our materials for movement. To start, it is best to have a grid to "fill in the blanks" for what we want to accomplish. Take a look at the example below. You can see that a week's worth of action-based goodies can be plugged in and viewed in a simple and easy-to-read table. And, there's also a reproducible grid to complete for easy access to the moves you want to include in your lessons. Let's look at the example of how you might view your week-at-a-glance (see Figure 7.1).

Figure 7.1   *Action-Packed Classrooms* Weekly Action Plan

Action-Packed Classrooms Weekly Action Plan	Week of: _____ _____ to _____		Class/Period:		
Day	Academic Integration	Music	Activities	Games	State Changes	Energizers
M						
T						
W						
TH						
F						

This is a very simple, easy-to-read format that can be adapted to anyone's needs. Hopefully you will find this beneficial in your planning at your school.

EVALUATING THE LESSON

Questions, questions, questions . . . hmm. Did the lesson work? Let's inquire to see if the planning was on target.

- Did students learn what you had hoped?
- Did all students learn something related to the content standards? How do you know?
- Did some new learning goals emerge during instruction?
- Can you evaluate your students' learning process as well as the products they created? Can you evaluate student proficiency in information access and student products/performances?
- What instructional strategies were the most effective?
- What one thing might you have done differently that would have made the lesson more effective?
- What else would you like to change next time you use this lesson?

Be sure to keep a log of your experiences so that next time, the lesson will be even more effective. You may also wish to collaborate on a regular basis with your colleagues, which will aid you in evaluating both your lesson and your students' work.

CHUNKING MOVEMENT *(Task Analysis)*

How and why does getting their attention or chunking matter when teaching movement-based activities? Simply put, it works! To help students remember progressions of movement such as juggling or dancing, break down the steps into sequences or chunks of movements; this process provides for better retention. Let's take a look at juggling.

When teaching juggling, it is advantageous to begin by grabbing three juggling scarves, tucking two in the waistband out of the way and holding on to the one. Why do we start with scarves? In movement, we want to progress from simplest to more complex. Scarves move very slowly as compared to balls, so it gives the learner ample time to learn the sequences of movements and allows for success.

The following is a sequence of steps for teaching juggling:

- One hand, one scarf juggling. Chunk this movement together—*toss the scarf up . . . catch it on top.* (So, the learner is keeping knuckles facing the sky.) After mastering that, continue to . . .
- Two hands, two scarves juggling. Chunk this movement together—*toss both scarves up, catch them on top.* (Keeping knuckles toward sky.) Next . . .

- Two hands, two scarves juggling. Chunk this movement together—*criss-cross, applesauce.* (Now we are crossing across the midline of the body.) Every time you say a word, you do an action. *Criss* . . . take one scarf from hip area and cross in front of body tossing up. *Cross* . . . take other scarf at other hip area and cross in front of body tossing up. *Apple* . . . catch the first scarf you let go of. And *sauce*, catch the second scarf. Continue with this pattern . . . *Criss-cross, applesauce* over and over.
- Two hands, three scarves juggling. Chunk this movement as well slipping in a third scarf. You still say *criss-cross, applesauce* as one scarf is always in limbo. Yes, you are now juggling!

As you can see, chunking the movement with words as you sequence the patterns works. It separates the movements into "learnable bits of info" where success can be attained by the majority. Another great example of chunking movement sequences is learning a line dance. Let's take a look!

The following is an example of the electric slide:

- Right, behind, right, touch (take right foot to the side, move left foot behind right, step with right foot, then bring left foot to right).
- Left, behind, left, touch (take left foot to the side, move right foot behind left, step with left foot, then bring right foot to left).
- Back, two, three, tap (step back on right foot, back on left foot, back on right foot, then tap left foot in front).
- Rock, two, three, swish (weight on right foot, weight on left foot, weight back on right foot, then swing right foot alongside left turning a quarter turn and facing now in a new direction).

Once learners have mastered the sequences in the electric slide as well as juggling, they just need to say the words and away they go!

- Criss-cross, applesauce
- Criss-cross, applesauce
- Criss-cross, applesauce
- Before you know it, you're juggling!

or try:

- Right, behind, right, touch
- Left, behind, left, touch
- Back, two, three, tap
- Rock, two, three, swish
- And repeat
- Before you know it, you're dancing!

Better yet, once the movements have been chunked together and the patterns become automatic, add some academic content to those movements. For example, try 1492 . . . Christopher Columbus sailed the blue . . . instead of criss-cross, applesauce. Or try some times tables to the electric slide. The sky's the limit! Chunking movement works.

GROUPING STUDENTS

Getting kids into groups, if not organized, can be an all-period ordeal. To maximize time and minimize inefficiency, let's take a look at these great ideas:

Index Cards With Stickers

Take index cards and put various stickers on them to form groups. For example, if you have 24 students, make one pack of cards with animal stickers that put students in eight groups of three. Examples are three rhinos, three lions, three monkeys, and so on. Shuffle the cards and walk around the room, allowing the students to pick a card. Let them look at their cards, but they shouldn't show anyone. Then, give the directions for the activity. After that, the students should get up and, WITHOUT talking, find the others in their group. After they find each other they bring the cards to the teacher. Bundle all of the cards up with a rubber band, and make a top card to tell you that the set is for eight groups of three. You can make other sets for other group configurations, such as five groups of four (one group has five). Once you make them up and label the cards, you can just pick which you want to use that day.

Deck of Cards

Use playing cards with students' names on them to randomly call on students. Take the playing cards, shuffle, and deal four cards. Those students are in a group. They actually like this! Of course not as much as them picking their own groups, but sometimes that is not feasible. They usually complete their work in a timely and efficient matter, and there are no feelings of animosity toward me. It's great.

UNO Cards

Randomly pass out UNO cards. You can have the students meet with people of the same number, the same color, or the same shape. Don't let them know in advance which you are going to choose to alleviate trading of cards.

Famous Pairs

For partner activities, make a set of index cards with famous up-to-date pairs on them. Pass them out to the students, and have them find their match. You can use names like Bert and Ernie, Fred and Wilma, Samson and Goliath, Robinson Crusoe and Friday, and so on. Update those who may become out-of-date each year and add popular ones to it. Also, have at least one if not more of a threesome in case you have an odd number of pupils attending that day. You could include Larry, Moe, Curly, and so on for this. The kids love to see who they get and then have to do a little thinking (novel idea) to find their match.

Puzzle Pieces

For each group, create a puzzle with the same number of pieces as students to be in that group. Paste a picture on a sheet of tagboard and laminate it. Cut the pieces apart, use a permanent marker to mark the number of students in the group on the back of the pieces, and store them in a resealable baggie. When it is time for a group activity, give students a puzzle piece. Then have them find the students with the rest of the puzzle.

No doubt about it, grouping students in an efficient manner can lead to a lot less headaches. I'm sure you will agree.

MAKE IT HAPPEN

To make standards-based instruction happen in your classroom, double-check that you are meeting the needs below.

Standards for Performance

What is the evidence of student learning or mastery? Think about the following:

- Is there more than one way to show mastery of this skill or concept? Do students have ample opportunity and means by which to master this standard?
- Do students know what a successful performance looks like?
- Do students know the criteria by which their performance will be evaluated up front?
- Are the criteria for mastery including action-based, intrinsic learning?
- Are all skills and concepts equally important—and given equal weight on any assessments?
- Is this method an effective and appropriate use of the teacher's time and attention?

Lay down a solid but adaptable foundation that will ensure the success of the lesson or unit once it begins. Although such attention to design asks a lot of the teacher at first, such questions and considerations become routine for designing instructional materials.

Teaching and Learning

Build on the learners' knowledge and progress by extending their capacity and competence as they move toward mastery of a standard.

Think about the following:

- Introduce the skill, concept, or task with clear instructions that students can hear, see, and do.
- Connect the lesson, concept, or unit to what they have studied or will study.
- Check for prior knowledge and current understanding of the skill or concept.
- Demonstrate the task, explaining what you are thinking as you do so.
- Try the task or explain their initial understanding of the concept.
- Evaluate their performance; check for understanding.
- Correct or clarify their performance as needed based on observed results.
- Practice the skill or continue study of the concept.
- Assess level of mastery and need for further group or individualized instruction.
- Extend students' understanding and mastery by increasing the difficulty of the task.
- Monitor students' level of mastery and need for further group or individualized instruction.
- Reinforce understanding and mastery through action-based, intrinsic activities.

LET'S WRAP IT UP

Now that the writing is on the wall and the proof is in the pudding, let's begin the process of evaluating all of this planning. Did all of the planning pay off? Are the kids getting the material in a more efficient manner? Am I, the teacher, less stressed out?

Planning that is geared toward assessment is imperative for checking for success. Without assessment, how do we know if learning occurred? As we take a journey through Chapter 8, we will look into assessment in detail and come away with some awesome ideas. Let's go!

8

Assessing Action-Packed Academics in Standards-Based Classrooms

Begin with the end in mind.

Once you have a clear picture of your priorities—that is values, goals, and high leverage activities—organize around them.

—Stephen Covey

LET'S BEGIN

Assessments come in many forms, from standard to more authentic. Assessments can be utilized in many ways. Once created, an established assessment can be used or slightly modified and applied to many activities. Reviewing, reconceptualizing, and revisiting the same concepts from different angles improve understanding of the lesson for students. A great example of an authentic assessment is using the rubric. Think about a movement rubric—good moves do not change with the project. Because the essentials remain constant, it is not necessary to create a completely new rubric for every activity. The experience students gain through an authentic project enables them to understand the various aspects necessary for creating a valuable piece of work.

129

Knowledge that has deep meaning provides the basis for students to judge objectively their own work as well as that of others. Developing a rubric is an example of a reflective process that extends the experience and the knowledge gained beyond simply turning in a project for a teacher-initiated grade.

CHECK THIS OUT

Teaching Language Arts

In Boise, Idaho, an elementary school teacher assesses her students grasp of the different parts of the English language through movement. For example, when being tested on verbs, the students act out the action of the word, or, better yet, they become action words. Based on a standards-based rubric, the children are assessed on their knowledge through their moves. What a great way to assess and anchor the learning of verbs!

Teaching Writing

North Dakota's Jefferson Elementary School implemented a new writing program after staff enrolled in for-credit courses on teaching writing as a process and integrating writing across content areas. Staff training also addressed cooperative learning, whole language learning, and assessment. Staff developed holistic scoring procedures to assess writing and document improvement over time. Assessment is ongoing in classrooms; students use feedback from classmates and teachers to assess and to improve performance. Conferences with partners and teachers, before and during writing, help students select topics and polish skills. Audiences are the class and the larger community: a Young Authors' Fair gave students opportunities to share their writing, illustrating, reading, and storytelling skills with parents and community members. In turn, local residents serve as role models by sharing their stories and poems with youngsters in school.

Teaching English

At a school in Medford, Oregon, seniors must complete a three-part senior project to graduate. Students first choose a topic of interest to them, conduct research, and write a paper. Then they use the information in the papers to create real-life projects. While these projects are used to satisfy requirements for senior English, the rich variety of topics chosen makes these efforts interdisciplinary. One aspiring singer wrote and performed (danced) a song that she had learned to orchestrate. Another student wrote about Big Brother and Big Sister programs and recruited students to work with children from broken homes. The third phase of the project is a formal, active presentation before a panel of faculty and community members, some of whom are experts in the topic. Following the formal action-based presentation, judges ask each senior several questions to evaluate impromptu speaking skills, knowledge level, comfort, and poise.

Teaching Social Studies

At Hope Middle School, Providence, Rhode Island, students in a sixth-grade class were assessed on plate tectonics by acting out and moving to the song "The Rock Cycle." They created, according to sixth-grade standards, an action-based test of plate tectonics, earthquakes, and so on—any kind of movement that matched up with the word. For example, many students were found on the floor wiggling around demonstrating the effects of an earthquake. I'm sure they'll never forget that assessment.

Teaching Science

Science teacher Cathy Klinesteker uses these closure activities for authentic assessment at Evergreen School in Cottonwood, California:

1. At the end of a unit, students write a paper for another class of students (younger, older, or the same age) explaining the concept. Example: Sixth graders write a book for fourth graders explaining the cycle of a star.

2. Cooperative groups of students do an artistic representation (poster, model, videotape, slide show, etc.) of a concept. Example: For a communication unit, students created a poster demonstrating their understanding of elements of communication, including nonverbal, questioning, paraphrasing, and empathy. The representation showed the interrelatedness and importance of each component.

3. Using equipment or a drawing (depending on the developmental stage of the students), students demonstrate understanding of a scientific principle such as an open electrical circuit; stream cutting during flood stage of a river; or a food web in the ocean, a pond, a desert, or a rain forest.

4. With partners, students prepare a debate demonstrating their understanding of two sides of a controversial issue.

Teaching Multiplication

At a second-grade class in Florida, kids were tested on their multiplication table or facts by doing the Macarena to each times table; for example, 4, 8, 12, 16, 20, and so on, with each hand movement. A rubric was created to check for understanding by completing the times tables to the music provided.

Teaching Math

In the Mendocino Middle School, Mendocino, California, math and science teacher Cory Wisnia's assessment strategies evaluate students' knowledge of a specific concept or subject area and the life skills they need for the future. One of the ways Wisnia teaches real-life skills in math and science classes is through projects that also can serve as final measures of learning. He teaches a unit or concept and then assigns projects that demonstrate how well students understand the concept. For example, to assess area and perimeter relationships in math, Wisnia asked the class to use a particular constant, "Say 1,250 square feet," and design a scale model of a dream home using graph paper for the floors. These strategies help Wisnia judge how much learning the student retained.

WHY EVEN BOTHER?

Many schools are designing and using innovative assessment strategies. Some of these techniques are called authentic assessment, performance-based assessment, portfolio assessment, process assessment, exhibits, demonstrations, and profiles. Regardless of the label, each of these techniques has moved beyond the concept of measuring student learning using multiple choice and other simple tests as single measures of student learning at one point in time.

WHAT IS ASSESSMENT?

As learning in schools is redefined, both the curriculum and the classroom environment need to be aligned. The collaborative classroom is characterized by shared knowledge among teachers and students, shared authority among teachers and students, teachers as mediators, and heterogeneous groupings of students.

Understanding where assessment planning occurs in the teaching-learning continuum provides a crucial insight into what makes standards-based instruction different from traditional classroom instruction. The paradigm shift requires that, prior to developing lesson plans, teachers determine what mastery of a standard looks like and select assessments that would provide evidence of mastery. Once assessments are selected, the skills, strategies, and activities needed to demonstrate mastery on the assessment are determined.

Assessment involves much more than end-of-chapter tests or quizzes on discrete skills and concepts. Assessments may involve student performances, demonstrations, and product development. They often involve real-world skills that encourage collaboration, action, critical thinking, and problem solving. Rubrics are often used to assess products and performances, because rubrics structure the levels of performance based on specific criteria. These criteria are often derived from the performance descriptors, standards, and benchmarks.

WHAT IS STANDARDS-BASED ASSESSMENT?

In standards-based education, ongoing assessment is critical to understanding how students are performing in relation to the selected standards. Formative assessment allows teachers to evaluate the effectiveness of instructional strategies, and potentially engages students in self-assessment. Formative assessments are woven throughout instruction and can be recorded at logical intervals in the flow of teaching and learning.

Content Standards

What should students know and be able to do by the end of this lesson, unit, or course? Think about the following:

- Connections to prior knowledge
- Constraints of time and resources
- Availability of necessary materials and resources

Student Preparation

What must students be able to do to accomplish? Think about the following:

- Specialized or new vocabulary terms
- Background knowledge
- Skills, capacities, habits, or techniques
- Connections to prior knowledge

Teacher Preparation

What does the teacher need to know to teach this skill or concept? Think about the following:

- What the teacher needs or wants to teach after this unit
- What support and material resources are available to help teach this skill or concept

Instructional Standards

What strategies and instructional designs are most effective and efficient in teaching this skill or concept? Think about the following:

- Graphic organizers
- Mind maps
- Note-making strategies
- Action-Packed instruction
- Reciprocal teaching, literature circles, direct instruction
- Class and student configurations
- Visual aids, multimodal, multisensory approaches

Curricular Conversations

How does this relate to other stuff? Think about the following:

- Workplace connections
- Personal connections
- Cross-curricular connections

Standards Alignment

Which standard? Think about the following:

- Curricular objectives and context of the lesson
- Current progress toward mastery of this standard
- Connections to and reinforcement of standards students have already met
- Standards you have not yet addressed or which students have not yet mastered

DIFFERENT ASSESSMENT STRATEGIES

The following definitions are put forth to help you better understand the various types of assessment:

Alternative Assessment

An alternative assessment is one that is different from those assessments that we normally give students (i.e., true/false, matching, essay questions, standardized tests, etc.). They are "untraditional" (i.e., drawing a picture, making a video of a particular skill, etc.). On many occasions this type of assessing allows students to create a product that the teacher will have to grade (usually using a rubric). Oftentimes students work with other classmates cooperatively.

Authentic Assessment

This is an assessment done in a "real-life" setting, as opposed to a more "sterile" testing situation. The instruction and assessment are both born out of situations from daily life. The more the assessment takes place in "real life," the more authentic it is.

Performance Assessment

A performance assessment is one in which students are asked to make, do, or create something—or, the 3 "P's": a performance task (doing something), product task, or portfolio task. Students actually create as opposed to just regurgitating answers on a test form.

Rubric

A rubric is a rating scale and list of criteria by which student knowledge, skills, or performance can be assessed.
What is a rubric, you ask?

- A rubric is a scoring guide that seeks to evaluate a student's performance based on the sum of a full range of criteria rather than a single numerical score.
- A rubric is an authentic assessment tool used to measure students' work.
- Authentic assessment is used to evaluate students' work by measuring the product according to real-life criteria. The same criteria used to judge a published author would be used to evaluate students' writing.

- Although the same criteria are considered, expectations vary according to one's level of expertise. The performance level of a novice is expected be lower than that of an expert and would be reflected in different standards. For example, in evaluating an activity, a first grader may not be expected to perform a movement to earn a high evaluation. A 10th grader would need to master the movement in order to earn high marks.
- A rubric is a working guide for students and teachers, usually handed out before the assignment begins in order to get students to think about the criteria on which their work will be judged.
- A rubric enhances the quality of direct instruction.

WHY USE RUBRICS?

Many experts believe that rubrics improve students' end products and therefore increase learning. When teachers evaluate activities, they know implicitly what makes a good final product and why. When students receive rubrics beforehand, they understand how they will be evaluated and can prepare accordingly. Developing a grid and making it available as a tool for students' use will provide the scaffolding necessary to improve the quality of their work and increase their knowledge.

Prepare rubrics as guides that students can use to build on current knowledge. Consider rubrics as part of your planning time, not as an additional time commitment to your preparation.

Once a rubric is created, it can be used for a variety of activities. Reviewing, reconceptualizing, and revisiting the same concepts from different angles improve understanding of the lesson for students. An established rubric can be used or slightly modified and applied to many activities.

There are many advantages to using rubrics:

- Teachers can increase the quality of their direct instruction by providing focus, emphasis, and attention to particular details as a model for students.
- Students have explicit guidelines regarding teacher expectations.
- Students can use rubrics as a tool to develop their abilities.
- Teachers can reuse rubrics for various activities.

Learning to create rubrics is like learning anything valuable. It takes an initial time investment. Once the task becomes second nature, it actually saves time while creating a higher quality student product.

The following criteria will help you get started:

- Determine the concepts to be taught. What are the essential learning objectives?
- Choose the criteria to be evaluated. Name the evidence to be produced.
- Develop a grid. Plug in the concepts and criteria.
- Share the rubric with students before they begin the activity.

Evaluate the end product. Compare individual students' activity with the rubric to determine whether they have mastered the content.

RUBRICS AND MOVEMENT

Rubrics can be created for any content area, including math, science, history, writing, foreign languages, drama, art, music, and, yes, even movement! Once developed, they can be modified easily for various grade levels. The following rubric is an example of a teacher-created rubric, but it could be developed easily by a group of elementary students (see Figure 8.1).

Figure 8.1   Movement Assessment

Movement

Dance

Partner Assessment

Direction: Please evaluate your partner and yourself using the following rubric:

Scoring #	What does it mean?
4	consistently/all of the time
3	usually/most of the time
2	occasionally/some of the time
1	rarely/seldom

What we are being tested on	Self	Partner
Knowledge of steps		
On count with music		
Enthusiasm while learning dance		
Provides "put-ups" to peers		
Does not give up		
Provided input on this checklist		

How did you do? _____

_____

Where in your community can you participate in this dance? _____

_____

Electric Slide Dance Rubric

The dance elements to judge include the following:

- Knowledge of steps
- On count with music
- Enthusiasm while learning dance
- Provides "put-ups" to peers
- Does not give up
- Provides input on checklist

4: Consistently

- Performed steps correctly three out of three attempts
- Fluid in movements
- Stayed to cadence
- Moved with rhythm
- Enthusiastic
- Provided positive input to peers
- Didn't quit

3: Usually

- Performed steps correctly two out of three attempts
- Showed some rhythm
- In line with cadence
- Somewhat fluid in movements
- Somewhat enthusiastic
- Somewhat positive input to peers
- Didn't quit

2: Occasionally

- Performed steps correctly one out of three attempts
- Needs improvement in step with rhythm
- Needs improvement with cadence
- Needs improvement with fluidity of movements
- Needs improvement with enthusiasm
- Needs improvement with positive input to peers
- Stayed on task some of the time

1: Rarely

- Performed steps correctly zero out of three attempts
- No rhythm
- No cadence

o No fluidity
o No enthusiasm
o No positive input
o Off task

Why should students create their own rubrics? Reading or listening to a teacher's expectations is very different for a student than creating and accomplishing his or her own goals. The purpose of inviting students to develop their own evaluation structure is to improve their motivation, interest, and performance in the project. As students' overall participation in school increases, they are likely to excel in it.

How can students create their own rubrics? Students are motivated intrinsically to design their own assessment tool after experiencing activity-based learning. Once students have invested a significant amount of time, effort, and energy into an activity, they naturally want to participate in deciding how it will be evaluated. The knowledge gained through experience in a particular activity, game, or dance provides the foundation for creating a useful rubric.

The experience students gain through an authentic project enables them to understand the various aspects necessary for creating a valuable piece of work. Knowledge that has deep meaning provides the basis for students to judge objectively their own work as well as that of others. Developing a rubric is a reflective process that extends the experience and the knowledge gained beyond simply turning in a project for a teacher-initiated grade.

TOWARD MULTIDIMENSIONAL ASSESSMENT

Given the truism that you "inspect what you expect," the message that continues to be sent to students is that only certain dimensions of learning are important. As different abilities and skills become increasingly valued in schools, new visions of assessment increasingly include assessment of the various abilities and skills.

Moving to a concept of "multidimensional assessment" means that evaluation of students will be based on a broader concept of intelligence, ability, and learning. Not only will logical and verbal abilities continue to be assessed, but assessment also will include kinesthetic, visual, auditory, intrapersonal, and interpersonal abilities. This means assessing students' repertoire of learning strategies, skills in communicating with others, and knowledge as it is applied to day-to-day and culturally diverse contexts.

Teaching and evaluation of student learning reflected in the term *multidimensional assessment* is broad based, relevant to real life, process oriented, action based, and based on multiple measures, which provide a rich portrayal of student learning.

Multidimensional assessment taps the power and diversity of active learning. *Action-Packed Classrooms* creates multiple sources of information to support instructional decision making and helps teachers become more effective teachers and students become more reflective and capable learners.

In implementing curriculums based on action, staff find that standardized tests are not usually useful in measuring the broad range of abilities fostered in the curriculum. Most tests measure only a narrow slice of children's linguistic and mathematical abilities. And even in these areas, the tests fail to reflect students' ability to think critically and creatively, their motivation to learn, or their capacity to engage in self-assessment.

Because of the limitations of standardized tests, teachers at various schools all over the world have to develop assessment strategies that will yield richer, more qualitative information about student achievement and instructional effectiveness.

Strategies include the following:

1. Videotaped portfolios document the learner's interests and accomplishments and assist teachers in evaluating each student's progress from year to year. The portfolios include tapes of an initial interview with the student and excerpts of his or her work throughout the year. Parents receive the videotape at the end of the year—it serves as a rich portrayal of their children's growth and an important supplement to information from report cards and results of standardized tests.

2. Each student keeps a journal with weekly entries about the school's themes and his or her projects.

3. Students spend a part of each week in a media-rich room where they can choose from a range of active exercises, mini projects, board games, puzzles, audio tapes, and other materials requiring the use of one or more of the seven abilities. A teacher observes and records which activities children select and how they tackle problems. That information will be combined with other evidence about the learner's interests and strengths to form a profile for each student.

4. Students also carry out an original project each nine-week grading period on a theme that encourages students to think across subject lines. Students are helped to assess their own projects by considering how well they illustrate the theme. These projects become part of the student's portfolio, documenting for both the teacher and the student his or her growth over time.

TEACHING TO THE TEST

Accompanying the move from a single test as a measure of student learning to multidimensional assessments has been a move to integrate assessment into the classroom instructional process. Viewing a test only as an "event" signaling completion of instruction is no longer appropriate for a vision that learning is a process

Figure 8.2   Revisions

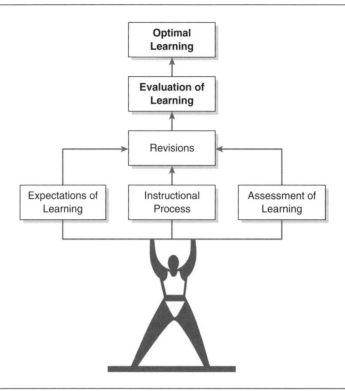

in which students orchestrate learning strategies in a dynamic flow as they move in and out of different lessons and phases of learning. Assessment, too, needs to be considered as an ongoing dynamic process.

Figure 8.2 shows assessment as part of a process that enables students to become successful learners. Assessment, in this graphic, becomes the feedback that enables students to be strategic in their own learning process and enables teachers to adapt the instructional process to meet the needs of their students. Assessment helps teachers communicate expectations and standards of learning and performance to students. Assessment helps students gain information about what is valued, set personal academic expectations, internalize the required knowledge and skills, promote their self-knowledge about performance, understand who is in control of learning, and improve their learning.

The direct linkage between expectations, instruction, and assessment is evident. The expectations for learning will drive both the instructional and assessment process. If it is important that expectations and assessment be linked, then it is also appropriate to say that a teacher should be teaching to the assessment given that assessment is authentic. Without a clear relationship between the two, neither students nor teachers can use assessment information to its greatest potential in promoting learning.

Examples of dynamic and ongoing assessments that enable teachers to modify instruction as needed are the techniques developed by Campione and Brown (1987).

Dynamic Assessment

The concept of dynamic assessment is a natural extension of the idea of integrating assessment and instruction. Teachers employing these techniques present students with increasingly explicit cues and prompts for performing a task.

Teachers may limit support by giving hints about the general approach to a particular problem, or they may need to provide a specific blueprint for solving a problem. The number of hints required for the student to solve each problem serves as a measure of learning efficiency. The fewer cues a teacher gives, the higher students' learning efficiency will be; the more cues a teacher gives, the lower students' learning efficiency will be. The assessment of learning efficiency focuses on how much help is needed for students to reach their learning potentials in a particular domain, rather than a static measure of what has already been acquired.

Assessment of Learning and Study Strategies

Weinstein, Schulte, and Palmer (1987) have constructed an instrument called the Learning and Studying Strategies Inventory (LASSI), which measures the use of strategies among secondary and postsecondary students. It identifies students' weaknesses and provides data on the effectiveness of training programs for students who have poor learning and study habits.

Students' attitude, motivation, time management, anxiety, concentration, information processing, study aids, self-testing, and test strategies are measured. The test focuses on modifiable behaviors in learning. For example, in the area of motivation, students are assessed on their diligence, self-discipline, and willingness to work hard. LASSI enables educators to help students become self-directed and self-managed learners.

MAKE IT HAPPEN

The "Standards-Based Assessment Checklist" (see Resources) is a great "cheat sheet" to organize assessment planning according to standards-based instruction and assessment. There are four phases to rotate through. When you accomplish and reach #4, you then rotate through and create new planning based on the results. Have fun!

LET'S WRAP IT UP

A broad vision for learning requires an educational environment where instruction and assessment are integrated and where assessment is not considered to be a single event. The concept of assessment as an active process in which students and teachers participate provides a model for new assessment techniques that are aligned with a multidimensional vision for teaching and learning.

9

Developing an Action Plan

I hear, I know. I see, I remember. I do, I understand.

—Confucius

LET'S BEGIN

In developing new strategies, it is important to build upon a firm foundation of research. *Action-Packed Classrooms* has substantiated through related literature the theoretic effectiveness of incorporating learning and brain-based research into a moving medium for classroom instruction. Given the overwhelming body of resources unearthed during this writing that support the use of brain-based research, instructional practices that incorporate movement activities, and increased activity, it is evident that this there is room to positively enhance current classroom instruction. The development of an instructional tool that is based on brain knowledge is justified by the literature; the research backs up this type of instruction, and it is loads of fun!

LET'S WRAP IT UP

Action-Packed Classrooms is divided into main sections. The sections are as follows:

- Understanding the effect of movement on learning
- Developing kinesthetic teaching strategies
- Developing an action plan . . . the how-tos

As you traveled through the first chapters of the book, you discovered about the body and the brain—vital information that is very important to making sense of what the research says regarding movement in the academic classroom as well as how to use movement and when it is appropriate. Ask yourself the following questions:

- Do I understand the basic functions of the brain and learning?
- Am I more sensitive to the issues of involvement, and am I getting my students more active?
- Can I explain to my colleagues why movement facilitates cognition?

Continuing along, you discovered incredible strategies for developing kinesthetic lessons for your academic classroom. Anchoring learning through procedural processes, you learned how exciting and fun the learning experience can be for you and your students. Ask yourself the following questions:

- Do I understand the learning hierarchy?
- Am I incorporating music into my classroom?
- Why is aerobic activity so important to academic brains?

Finally, you put together an action plan. Ask yourself the following questions:

- Am I taking care of my stress levels?
- Do I create clear learning objectives for my students?
- Am I moving toward multidimensional assessments?

As we conclude this book, hopefully you are "filled to the brim" with a wealth of information and tools to fire up your classroom and bring learning alive. Many factors come into play when teaching. With all of the research exploding in favor of more engagement by the learner, it does not make sense to leave out action no matter what other factors you may incur. Instead of viewing learners as spectators of education, teachers need to ensure that learners are participating in the learning process. As the old saying goes, "If you always do what you always did, you'll always get what you always got." Today is the first day of the rest of our lives. Why not make this the best year ever?

Questions upon questions: Do we understand the research behind movement and learning? Did we learn strategies to anchor learning in any classroom? Did we create an "Action Plan" to build on current lessons to make instruction come alive? Do we have "good-to-go" activities to immediately implement in the classroom? *Action-Packed Classrooms* is not the total solution, but it can have a significant impact on the overall productivity of a class's academic performance. This book does so by showing teachers how to use specific strategies to stimulate the multiple intelligences by engaging students in dynamic ways.

Since teaming up with another teacher or your whole school implementing *Action-Packed Classrooms*, did you make sure that the skills you mastered became an inherent part of your teaching style? Embrace the *Action-Packed Classroom* teaching techniques because they are proven to work—you can't go wrong!

Finally, revisit and review your pledge with the commitment contract, and finish the year collaborating with your colleagues. You will be amazed at seeing the increase in learning in your students and the decrease in your frustration as a teacher.

Congratulations on the successful completion of this book; I hope it will have a big impact on your teaching career. I have no doubt that with *Action-Packed Classrooms*, you will enjoy many more successful years to come.

Resources

Make-It-Happen Checklist for Movement in Your Classroom

#	Movement Facilitation	Scoring Criteria	Score
1	Integrating Movement and Academics: A._____ B._____ C._____	(Chapter 4) 3 integrations per week = 3 2 integrations per week = 2 1 integrations per week = 1 0 integrations per week = L	
2	Moving Through the Disciplines With Cadence and Music: A._____ B._____ C._____	(Chapter 5) 3 music/moves per week = 3 2 music/moves per week = 2 1 music/moves per week = 1 0 music/moves per week = L	
3	Jump-Start With Energizers and Attention Grabbers A._____ B._____ C._____	(Chapter 6) 3 energizers per week = 3 2 energizers per week = 2 1 energizers per week = 1 0 energizers per week = L	
4	Aerobic Recess and Classroom Teachers PE–Lifesavers A._____ B._____ C._____	(Chapter 7) 3 aerobic fun per week = 3 2 aerobic fun per week = 2 1 aerobic fun per week = 1 0 aerobic fun per week = L	
5	Personal New Great Ideas to Fire Up Learning A._____ B._____ C._____	(Whatever Floats Your Boat) Give Yourself Bonus Points! 3 new ideas per week = 3 2 new ideas per week = 2 1 new ideas per week = 1	

Scoring Guide: 10–12 points—Awesome!   Total Score:
7–9 points—Looking Good!
4–6 points—Alrighty Now!
0–3 points—Hmmmm.

Measuring Up Worksheet

Name: _____   Grade: _____   Date: _____

1. Rope:

    _____ feet long

    _____ feet/yardstick measurement

    _____ inches

    _____ yards

2. Hoop:

    _____ feet long

    _____ feet/yardstick measurement

    _____ inches

    _____ yards

3. The hoop is _____ than the rope.

    a. Less than (<)

    b. Greater than (>)

    c. Equal to (=)

    d. Not sure

Movement Reminders Checklist for Academic Action

#	Movement Reminders	Criteria	Yes/No
1	Age-Level Specification: A. _____ B. _____ C. _____	Because of the varied abilities and uniqueness of each and every student, the activities are geared for most grade levels. You will have to be the judge of that as you peruse through these academic reinforcers, asking yourself, "Will this work with my kids?"	
2	Equipment/Facility Issues: A. _____ B. _____ C. _____	Because most of teachers out there in "teacherland" don't have equipment for a multiple of reasons, the activities are flexible enough to use "whatever works." Instead of poly spots, paper plates have been substituted. Of course, if you have poly spots, use them! Regarding facilities, every school is different. Adapt. If there is a will, there is a way.	
3	Safety Issues: A. _____ B. _____ C. _____	When substituting such things as paper plates versus poly spots, safety is of utmost importance. You may end up with a big owee! As for other homemade or substitutions for equipment, think safety first.	
4	Creativity: A. _____ B. _____ C. _____	Do what works for you. There may be a game or activity that you need to tweak to make it happen with your kids. Do whatever it takes to make learning come alive for you, and don't be afraid to add your unique touch to it.	
5	Music: A. _____ B. _____ C. _____	Whenever possible, include music. Music is a very powerful hook into any activity as it just makes it more fun. In many subject matter activities, there is music that is a subject-matter match for the activity. Do whatever you can to reinforce the academia. The game descriptors do not tell you to use music and a boom box when figuring out "what stuff do we need?" Ask yourself, "What music could I use here?"	

Recess/Physical Education Checklist for Aerobic Brains

#	(1) Recess/PE	(2) Facilities	(3) Equipment
1	Warm-Up Activities: A. _____ B. _____ C. _____	A. _____ B. _____ C. _____	A. _____ B. _____ C. _____
2	Aerobic Tag Games: A. _____ B. _____ C. _____	A. _____ B. _____ C. _____	A. _____ B. _____ C. _____
3	Inside/Playground Games: A. _____ B. _____ C. _____	A. _____ B. _____ C. _____	A. _____ B. _____ C. _____
4	Outside/Field Games: A. _____ B. _____ C. _____	A. _____ B. _____ C. _____	A. _____ B. _____ C. _____
5	Basketball and Water Fun: A. _____ B. _____ C. _____	A. _____ B. _____ C. _____	A. _____ B. _____ C. _____

Standards-Based Unit Planner

1. Decide what state content standard(s) will be taught in the unit.

State Content Standard

2. Choose a performance standard that will demonstrate mastery of the content standards. Describe the final product.

Performance Standard	Final Product Description

3. Develop a rubric (Chapter 8) describing products that meet and exceed the standards.

Meets the Standard What evidence will show that this student has met the standards taught in this unit?	Exceeds the Standard What evidence will show that this student has exceeded the standards taught in this unit?

4. Assess (Chapter 8) what knowledge is needed to achieve mastery of the standards. Figure out what your students already know and what they need to learn for success.

Prior Knowledge	New Knowledge

(Continued)

(Continued)

5. Based on what students need to learn, create learning chunks.

Knowledge Needed	Standards Addressed	Description of Learning Chunk

Standards-Based Assessment Checklist

#	*Standards-Based Assessment*	*Process to Accomplish Tasks*
1	Curriculum	
2	Assessment	
3	Instruction	
4	Analysis	

References

Allen, R. (2001). *Train smart*. San Diego, CA: The Brain Store.

Campione, J. C., & Brown, A. L. (1987). *Dynamic assessment: An interactional approach to evaluating learning potential* (pp. 82–115). New York: Guilford.

Hickey, D. T. (2003). Engaged participation versus marginal nonparticipation: A stridently socio-cultural approach to achievement motivation. *The Elementary School Journal, 103*(4), 401–431.

Hitzig, E., & Fritsch, G. (1870). Uber die elektrische erregbarkeit des grosshirns [The localized electrical excitability of the cerebral hemispheres]. *Archiv für Anatomie, Physiologie, und Wissenschaftliche Medizin, 37*, 300–332.

Jensen, E. (2003). *Tools for engagement*. Thousand Oaks, CA: Corwin.

Kindler, A. M. (2003). Visual culture, visual brain, and (art) education. *Studies in Art Education, 44*(3), 290–297.

Molteni, R., Wu, A., Vaynman, S., Ying, Z., Barnard, R. J., & Gomez-Pinilla, F. (2004). Exercise reverses the harmful effects of consumption of a high-fat diet on synaptic and behavioral plasticity associated to the action of brain-derived neurotrophic factor. *Neuroscience, 123*(2), 429–440.

Ratey, J. (2008). *Spark: The revolutionary new science of exercise and the brain*. New York: Little, Brown and Company.

Sylwester, R., & Cho, J. Y. (1993). What brain research says about paying attention. *Educational Leadership, 50*(4), 71–75.

Weinstein, C. E., Schulte, A. C., & Palmer, D. R. (1987). *Learning and Study Strategies Inventory (LASSI)*. Clearwater, FL: H & H Publishing.

List of Activities

CORWIN
A SAGE Company

The Corwin logo—a raven striding across an open book—represents the union of courage and learning. Corwin is committed to improving education for all learners by publishing books and other professional development resources for those serving the field of PreK–12 education. By providing practical, hands-on materials, Corwin continues to carry out the promise of its motto: **"Helping Educators Do Their Work Better."**